P9-DUU-281

AMERICA'S POLITICAL DYNASTIES

ADVANCE READING COPY
THESE ARE UNCORRECTED PAGE PROOFS.
PLEASE CHECK ALL QUOTES AND CITATIONS AGAINST THE FINISHED BOOK.

AMERICA'S POLITICAL DYNASTIES

From Adams to Clinton

STEPHEN HESS

BROOKINGS INSTITUTION PRESS

Washington, D.C.

Copyright © 2016
THE BROOKINGS INSTITUTION
1775 Massachusetts Avenue, N.W., Washington, D.C. 20036
www.brookings.edu

All rights reserved. No part of this publication may be reproduced or transmitted in any form or by any means without permission in writing from the Brookings Institution Press.

Unless otherwise noted, all images are reproduced from the collections of the Library of Congress.

The Brookings Institution is a private nonprofit organization devoted to research, education, and publication on important issues of domestic and foreign policy. Its principal purpose is to bring the highest quality independent research and analysis to bear on current and emerging policy problems. Interpretations or conclusions in Brookings publications should be understood to be solely those of the authors.

Library of Congress Cataloging-in-Publication data is available.
ISBN 978-0-8157-2708-8 (cloth : alk. paper)
ISBN 978-0-8157-2710-1 (epub)
ISBN 978-0-8157-2711-8 (pdf)

Typeset in Adobe Caslon

Composition by Elliott Beard

For Beth

CONTENTS

AMERICA'S
POLITICAL
DYNASTIES

ONE

THE DYNASTIC IMPULSE

MY FASCINATION WITH AMERICA's political families began, improbably, in Frankfurt, Germany, 1957. I was an army private stationed at the Third Armored Division headquarters. One evening I went to the library hoping to find something entertaining and instead spied a behemoth titled *The Biographical Directory of the United States Congress,* listing every legislator since the Continental Congress of 1774. As I skimmed names, some kept reappearing, repeated over and over. Muhlenberg. Muhlenberg. Muhlenberg. Muhlenberg. Bayard. Bayard. Bayard. Bayard. Stocktons and Frelinghuysens. Who were these senators and congressmen I had never heard of?

I had had a good education. I was a political science major! I knew of the Presidents Adams, John and John Quincy, father and son, and the two Roosevelt presidents, Theodore and Franklin, fifth cousins. I even knew about the Harrisons, having helped a professor research a history of the Republican Party. But who were these Livingstons, Breckinridges, and Tuckers? Or the Washburns, four brothers who had served in Congress from Maine, Illinois, Minnesota, and Wisconsin?

The Constitution declares, "No title of nobility shall be granted by the United States." Yet in the two centuries since these words were written, Americans had apparently chosen what Stewart Alsop once called "the People's Dukes."

Generation after generation, voters freely turned to the same families. Yet students of politics at the time were paying little attention to this phenomenon. When the army sent me home in 1958, replacing me with Elvis Presley (at least in the sense that his unit moved in when my unit moved out), I had compiled 300 genealogies. Someday I would tell their stories.

Many of these dynasties were ancient, having emerged, then faded away, so long ago. There hadn't been a Randolph of Virginia in Congress since 1833, a Winthrop of Massachusetts since 1851. Then in 1960, surprisingly, shockingly, the Kennedys arrived on the presidential scene with a talent so bright as to light up the sky. Jack told a New York audience he had received a wire from his father: "Dear Jack: Don't buy one vote more than necessary. I'll be damned if I'll buy a landslide." John Fitzgerald Kennedy, the dutiful son, narrowly won, and moved into the White House with a beautiful young wife and two engaging children who would play games under the president's desk. He made his brother Bob his attorney general. Brother Ted was soon installed in Jack's old Senate seat. Sargent Shriver, a brother-in-law, came to Washington to create the Peace Corps. Plus there was a bevy of sisters married to movie stars or British lords.

Suddenly, America's dynastic impulse became worth considering and might even have consequences for a democracy. In 1966, the year I turned my Frankfurt notes into the first edition of *America's Political Dynasties*, the U.S. Senate had eighteen members who were in some manner dynastically connected. Across the Capitol, in the U.S. House of Representatives, there were eleven sons of congressmen, two sons of senators, four who had had brothers in Congress, three whose husbands had been in Congress, and a slew of others with more distant relatives. Their stories were ripe for the telling.

SHORTLY BEFORE HIS THIRTY-SECOND birthday, in 2012, Joseph P. "Joe" Kennedy III was elected to the U.S. House of Representatives. A Harvard Law graduate, class of 2009, he was an assistant DA in the Middlesex County District Attorney's Office when he resigned to seek a congressional seat, winning the Democratic primary with a name worthy of 90 percent of the vote and the general election with 61 percent. He is the son of Joseph P. Kennedy II, who also served in the U.S. House of Representatives from Massachusetts in 1987 to 1999. Joseph P. Kennedy II is the eldest son of Robert F. Kennedy, the U.S. senator from New York who was murdered while running for the Democratic presidential nomination in 1968, and a nephew of President

John F. Kennedy and Senator Ted Kennedy, as well as a cousin of Patrick J. Kennedy, Ted's son, who was a member of the U.S. House of Representative from Rhode Island in 1995 to 2011. Joe Kennedy is now the sixth Kennedy to have been elected to Congress, a remarkable achievement for any family and amazing for one that entered Congress only in 1947.

Forty-four American political families have had at least four members of the same name elected to federal office, and in seventy-five families three members of the same name held national office. Another forty-eight dynasties could be called "mix and match" because they produced three or more members joined through marriage, such as the Rockefellers with the Aldriches. Yet collectively, these dynastic families, though unique, have contributed just 6 percent of the men and women who have been elected to Congress since 1774.

This book is the story of seventeen of these families, plus another family of two, who may be in the process of redefining dynasty. From these eighteen families have come eleven presidents, four vice presidents, thirty-three senators, eighteen governors, seventy-three members of the U.S. House of Representatives or Continental Congress, and eleven cabinet officers.

Although these families are bound together by their pursuit of the same goal, winning elections, their histories are as varied as the Adamses' and the Lees'. The first Adams left his heirs a house, a barn, and three beds; the first Lee left an estate of 13,000 acres, all rich tobacco land. With little in common, they joined together to maneuver America's separation from Great Britain and a revolution.

Politics was a by-product of religion for the Muhlenbergs and Frelinghuysens. Reverend Henry Melchior Muhlenberg had been sent to Pennsylvania by the German Lutheran Church. Reverend Theodorus Jacobus Frelinghuysen had been sent to New Jersey by the Dutch Reformed Church. By the time of the American Revolution, Germans made up a third of Pennsylvania's population and Dutch a sixth of New Jersey's—sizable voting blocs indeed!

Not all the founders were as patriotic as the Adamses and Lees or as pious as the Muhlenbergs and Frelinghuysens. The first Livingston was charged with pulling off "one of the grossest land frauds ever perpetrated in an age noted for unethical dealings." The first Lodge forefather in the Senate turned the American Revolution into a good thing financially as a privateer.

The Roosevelts, until the arrival of TR and FDR in the eighth generation, were two branches of moderately successful shopkeepers, bankers, and minor landed gentry, with hardly a politician among them. The brilliant Tuckers in Virginia arrived at politics secondary to the study and teaching of law. *Tucker on Blackstone. Tucker on the Constitution.* No one ever accused the Harrisons of brilliance. Their hallmark was adaptability. They went wherever they could find voters—Virginia, Indiana, Ohio, Illinois, and finally Wyoming.

Otherwise, dynasties tended to stay in a single state as they advanced generation after generation. *The Tafts of Ohio. The Bayards of Delaware.* They crossed borders when their ambitions exceeded a state's needs. *The Kennedys of Massachusetts, New York, Rhode Island, Maryland, Connecticut.* The Bushes have their own Connecticut-Texas-Florida history in this regard.

Within the dynasties there was harmony, until there was not. The Hyde Park Roosevelts and the Oyster Bay Roosevelts were destined to come into conflict. The Civil War split the Kentucky Breckinridges exactly down the middle, and no Louisiana Long was ever going to wait in line behind another Long. Yet there could also be deep family regard. The newspaper publisher Charlie Taft personally financed the long public career of his brother, William Howard Taft. Washburn of Wisconsin, on the floor of the House of Representatives in 1858, came to the defense of his brother from Illinois, grabbing Elihu's attacker by the hair. (It was a wig, and came off in Washburn's hands.)

All the dynasties without exception engaged in uncommon combat in America's wars. Jack Kennedy and George H. W. Bush fought in World War II, and Teddy Roosevelt's sons and grandsons became known for remarkable feats in both world wars. Robert E. Lee was the greatest general of them all, while on the Union side, Ben Harrison, unassertive as president, displayed bravery beyond courage during Sherman's March to the Sea. Robert Field Stockton fought in California during the Mexican War (and earned the honor of having a city named after him), while a century of schoolchildren were taught about young pastor Peter Muhlenberg marching from his church door into the Continental Army to fight with Washington at Valley Forge.

There were the great achieving families—the Adamses, Lees, Roosevelts, Tafts, Bushes, Clintons—and others more interesting than important. Still, there were great moments: James A. Bayard, Delaware's lone congressman in 1801, broke with his party to vote for Jefferson over Burr when the presidency had to be decided in the House of Representatives; Robert A. Livingston was U.S. minister to France during the years when the Louisiana Purchase was considered, then formally effected; Elihu B.

Washburne, another U.S. minister to France, was the only diplomat to remain in Paris during the Franco-Prussian War, supervising the relief of 30,000 people; Henry St. George Tucker was the author of the Seventeenth Amendment to the Constitution, which provides for the direct election of senators.

Dynastic accounting must also measure the critical role of women in their success. A framed photograph of Eleanor Roosevelt sat on a table in Hillary Clinton's White House office. Mrs. Clinton quotes Mrs. Roosevelt in her memoirs: "A woman is like a teabag. You never know how strong she is until she's in hot water." Abigail Adams proved so skillful in commerce and as a farm manager when her husband, John, was in France during the Revolution that she alone restored the family to solvency. Martha Bowers, Robert Taft's wife, was such an adept campaigner (as he was not) that a Cleveland newspaper announced his upset victory in 1938 under the headline "BOB AND MARTHA TAFT ELECTED TO THE SENATE." Edward Livingston, the minister to France, in his old age wrote to his wife, "What I am, my dear Louise, I owe chiefly to you." This is a common theme in this story of male office-seekers.

Yet unfortunately, the story of their children was too often one of alcoholism, drug addiction, mental illness, mental retardation, financial reverses or misconduct, sex scandals, or an inability to bear the burdens of their celebrity. Abigail and John had one son who became president of the United States and another who killed himself. John F. Kennedy Jr. called two of his first cousins, in print, "poster boys for bad behavior. . . .To whom much is given much is expected, right?" No dynasty children so abused their inheritance as the three eldest sons of FDR and Eleanor. Elliott, between 1934 and 1977, was investigated at least eight times by congressional committees. A Herblock cartoon showed FDR Jr., who had represented Rafael Trujillo of the Dominican Republic in Washington, sitting on a pile of the dictator's money. The caption read, "I'm broadminded—I'm just as willing to work for a democracy."

There were also in-laws. As in many families, some were unusual. Nicholas Bayard married a woman who was imprisoned for being a witch. In 1662 Judith Verlet was "seized in a strange manner with Fits." Fortunately, Nicholas's uncle was the New York governor Peter Stuyvesant, and his letter to Connecticut governor John Winthrop settled the matter. In the Stockton family, Rebecca married a man who was said to have been dead for four days and who, after returning to life, gave an account of heaven. Rebecca's sister Susanna married one of General Washington's spies. A Livingston in-law was Robert Fulton, inventor of the steamboat, which was to the financial advantage of the family. An elderly Frelinghuysen in-law led a suffrage march to the White House in 1919, for which she spent a night in jail. She reported that "the gas vapors from the sewers escaped. The fumes from the furnace escaped. Everything escaped but the prisoners."

The families were Protestant, except for the Catholic Kennedys and a branch of the Bushes; they were usually rich, at death if not at birth, although not "as rich as a Rockefeller" (unless they were Rockefellers). During the age of the robber barons and Mrs. Astor's "Four Hundred," there were no Astors, Vanderbilts, Goulds, Morgans, or Harrimans in Congress. Jay Gould felt political influence was best purchased when needed. They were not adverse, however, to their daughters marrying politicians, creating a special source of dynastic wealth: the advantageous marriage. In 1901 the son of John D. Rockefeller, the richest man in America, married the daughter of Senator Nelson Aldrich, the most powerful politician in America. Their son, Nelson Aldrich Rockefeller, became vice president of the United States. In the same way wealth also came to the Adamses, Tafts, and Frelinghuysens. A dynastic family generally was large. Philip Lee had seventeen children. John Scott Harrison, whose father and son were presidents, had thirteen. The Kennedys would not have had a fifth and sixth generation in Congress had Robert and Ethel not had eleven children. Having an only child can limit dynasty building.

I find the family the most mysterious and fascinating institution in the world, writes novelist Amos Oz.

SIX OF THESE DYNASTIES ended in the nineteenth century, and several others were on life support after 1900. Perhaps more is to be learned about the nature of dynasties by asking why they leave politics. (Why they get started in politics usually owes to some meshing of ambition, circumstance, and patriotism.)

The Adamses had several explanations for their political demise. John could have contended that it was a planned exodus. While serving in France, he wrote Abigail, "I must study politics and war that my sons may have liberty to study mathematics and philosophy. My sons ought to study mathematics and philosophy . . . in order to give their children a right to study painting, poetry, music, architecture." This theory of politics to poetry in three generations turned out to be a fairly accurate prediction for the Adams family. "A single family can stay adjusted through three generations," Brooks Adams claimed. "It is now full four generations since John Adams wrote the Constitution of Massachusetts. It is time that we perished. The world is tired of us." He was right in that the flinty Adamses had become more and more out of step with what voters wanted in their politicians.

If the people rejected the Adamses, the Livingstons rejected the people. "I should find myself ill-calculated to take a lead among men rendered fastidious by too much courtship, to intrigue with little men," answered a Livingston when asked why he had left the political scene. When the Livingstons could no longer control politics, they retired to their country estates, married other Livingstons, had fewer children, and got their income from investments rather than from entrepreneurial activities. Maintaining the status quo became a full-time occupation.

The Lees of Virginia stayed in politics for a while after the Civil War. Fitzhugh Lee was governor from 1885 until 1890. But his two sons became cavalry officers and his three daughters married army officers (all generals), and after that they were all naval officers or daughters married to generals' sons. Vice Admiral Fitzhugh Lee was skipper of the carrier *Manila Bay* during the battle for Leyte Gulf. The family had transformed itself into a military dynasty. The Civil War also had an impact on the careers of the Breckinridges, as some of them saw better opportunities available outside the war-torn South and left Kentucky, the seat of their political power.

Only the Frelinghuysens stayed in place. The sixth of the family in Congress, Rodney, today represents the Raritan Valley of New Jersey as his father, Peter, had before him. It is the land where the congressman's great-great-great-great-great-great grandfather, Theodorus Jacobus Frelinghuysen, settled in January 1720.

Dynasties die, and new dynasties are created, such as the Udalls. Stewart was first elected to Congress from Arizona in 1954. He was succeeded by his brother, Mo, after President Kennedy appointed him secretary of the interior in 1961. In the next generation, Stewart's son Tom was elected to the U.S. House in 1998 and to the Senate in 2008, representing New Mexico, and Mo's son Mark was similarly elected to the U.S. House in 1998 and to the Senate in 2008, representing Colorado. Mark, however, was defeated when he ran for reelection in 2014.

The rise and fall of dynasties was on display in the 2014 midterm elections. Besides Mark Udall, others from well-known families who lost Senate races were Mark Begich of Alaska, Mark Pryor of Arkansas, Kay

Hogan of North Carolina, Michelle Nunn of Georgia, and Mary Landrieu of Louisiana. There was a winner: Shelly Moore Caputo, daughter of a West Virginia governor, moved from the House to the Senate. Mary Landrieu's brother was reelected mayor of New Orleans. President Carter's grandson was defeated in his race for governor of Georgia. Gwen Graham, a new member of the U.S. House of Representatives as of 2014, is the daughter of former Senator Bob Graham; and John Dingell, who inherited his seat from his father in 1955, gave up the seat so that his wife Debbie could successfully succeed him.

There will always be dynasties. They will not always be the same ones.

America is a land of past and future dynasties. In this fluid game of getting to dynasty, there is no shortage of applicants. Public service is a worthy goal, and the routes to the top are carefully marked out. One may rise by climbing an elective-office ladder, from city, to state, to Washington, or jump the queue through celebrity status, war heroes preferred, but athletes and actors will do. Ethnic groups need a critical mass and a location from which to stake a claim. Just as the Muhlenbergs worked from a Pennsylvania Dutch power base in the late eighteenth century and the Kennedys followed the Irish to Boston a hundred years later, Little Italy in Baltimore sent Thomas D'Alesandro successively to the Maryland legislature, the Baltimore City Council, the U.S. Congress, and back to the mayor's office. His son also was mayor, and his daughter, Nancy Pelosi, became Speaker of the U.S. House of Representatives. Groups that disperse widely, such as Americans from India, are disadvantaged.

A brand name is a valuable asset—until it isn't—especially in a small state. For half the years between 1804 and 1929, a Bayard represented Delaware in the Senate. Voters can make pre-decisions based on past experiences with a dynastic family—it is comforting and efficient—and if they are wrong, there's always the next election. Congress is full of those who got there largely because their fathers or husbands got there first and then died in office. It would be generous to consider merely father-son or even grandmother-grandson (of which there is one case) relations to be a dynasty, although the media love the word and the temptation. As Diane Kincaid Blair wrote in *Over His Dead Body*, "For women aspiring to serve in Congress, the best husband has been a dead husband, most preferably one serving in Congress at the time of his demise." And as David Brooks has noted, "Now that women are more empowered, each dominant clan has essentially doubled the size of its talent pool, so family influence is increased." Voters seem to give heirs one free pass, a step up the elective ladder, before the newcomers must prove themselves. Two of FDR's sons won seats in the House of Representatives but were defeated when they tried to climb higher.

From the last two decades of the twentieth century into the next decades of the twenty-first, when the political landscape in the United States appears dominated by two families, there are some who are embarrassed or made uncomfortable by what they perceive as an antidemocratic slide toward government-by-legacy. Or perhaps they just don't like one or the other of the contenders, and blame the American two-party system. What is fascinating about the Bushes and the Clintons in terms of background, style, and personality is that they have nothing in common except a burning desire to get elected president of the United States. A nice irony is that while the Clintons are not a dynasty but would like to be one, the Bushes are a dynasty but deny that they are one.

So one lesson of this study is patience: this too shall pass. A democracy means that any citizen—now male or female—can try to start his or her own dynasty. And as this study shows, many do. The people who try are ambitious and energetic. Some have advantages—life isn't fair. Some have changed history, others have had modest effect. On average, in this opinion, collectively they have been above average. The end result is that America's political dynasties, rather than representing rigidity (as the word "dynasty" might imply), are part of the flux, the rise and fall, of a constantly changing scene.

TWO

THE
Adams
DYNASTY

I feel that the Adams family intimidates us all.
—JOHN F. KENNEDY[1]

It would be difficult to find in history another case of four successive generations of intellectual distinction and highest public service
equal to that shown by the Adams family during the past century
and a half.

—HENRY CABOT LODGE SR.[2]

THE INHERITANCE OF AN Adams includes a standard set of physical characteristics. It is as if a die had stamped out assembly-line
face and body parts. The Adams frame is short and stocky. (John
Adams, when vice president, was referred to as "His Rotundity.") The
Adams face, from top to bottom, has a tendency to baldness, a broad fore-
head, finely arched eyebrows, penetrating eyes, a slightly aquiline nose, and
a bulldog jaw.

Each Adams also inherited an uncommonly constant collection of personality traits. To the observing public, the typical Adams was tactless, often
beyond the point of rudeness; lacking in humor; introspective, sometimes
morbidly so; preachy, scholarly, and moralistic; austere, cold, and unsocial.

Tactlessness, an overwhelming political liability for most mortals, was a

11

"prenatal manner" to an Adams—"congenital, hereditary and in the blood," according to the second Charles Francis Adams.[3] In 1782 Sir John Temple said of John Adams, "He is the most ungracious man I ever saw."[4] And James Russell Lowell later remarked, "The Adamses have a genius for saying even a gracious thing in an ungracious way!"

No one was more aware of an Adams failing than an Adams. Through diaries, autobiographies, and letters they practiced self-flagellation of the soul. John Quincy Adams thought himself "a man of reserved, cold, austere, and forbidding manners; my political adversaries say, a gloomy misanthropist, and my personal enemies, an unsocial savage."[5] These were the same family traits that caused Governor Marcus Morton of Massachusetts to call Charles Francis Adams "the Greatest Iceberg in the Northern hemisphere."[6]

Yet within his intimate circle, an Adams was often able to display considerable conviviality. At a New York dinner party in the late 1830s the host served fourteen different madeiras, and John Quincy Adams surprised and delighted his companions by correctly identifying eleven of them.[7] Henry Adams, though an eccentric recluse to the world in general, was a devoted and cherished part of a particular social world that included John Hay, Theodore Roosevelt, and Henry Cabot Lodge Sr. Hay was fond of calling Henry "Porcupinus Angelicus." And clearly, for four generations the Adams prickly exterior was a protective armor to cover a morbidly sensitive interior.

As politicians, the Adamses stood before the people but were never of the people. They did not know how to be popular. When an inebriated voter said to President John Quincy Adams, "I hope the Constitution may never be broken," the president stiffly replied, "I concur heartily in that wish and hope that *your* constitution may never be broken."[8] It was not meant as a joke; he simply did not know how to cope with the intoxicating banter of the hustings. In New York in 1826, Charles Francis Adams was amazed to find among his father's supporters "an attachment to him amounting even to enthusiasm." He quickly explained to himself: "Perhaps the wine produced as much of this as anything else."[9]

It has been long lives, not any deliberate acts on their part, that brought the Adamses whatever public popularity they received from their contemporaries. In the public mind, old age bestows lovability on a politician. And longevity was an Adams characteristic. The average life span of the seven most famous members of the dynasty was more than eighty-two years.

John Adams, 1735–1826

THE ADAMSES ROSE TO prominence over the strenuous objections of the leading citizens of Massachusetts, their home state, and without the necessary financial means to support the occupation of public servant in a republic.

Ironically, the dynasty, now synonymous with Proper Boston, spent its most productive years at odds with the Back Bay elite. The Adamses of Quincy started on "the wrong side of Boston's narrow-gauge social tracks," wrote social arbiter Cleveland Amory.[10] When John Adams entered Harvard College in 1751 he was ranked socially fifteenth in a class of twenty-four; he would have rated even lower had his mother not been a Boylston. Politically, he and Sam Adams were for independence, which was against the better judgment of State Street; John Quincy Adams was for union and against the Hartford Convention; Charles Francis Adams was for abolition. For three generations the Adamses were almost perversely opposed to whatever Boston's leading merchants felt was in their best interests. It would have been asking a saintly dose of charity to forgive the Adamses for their hundred years of being "right." Small wonder that Henry Adams, in the fourth generation, could write of his family's "inherited quarrel with

State Street."[11] Or that his brother Charles Francis could write, "I have tried Boston socially on all sides; I have summered it and wintered it, tried it drunk and tried it sober; and, drunk or sober, there's nothing in it—save Boston!"[12]

They were a family that lacked the financial underpinnings to support their very considerable zest for public service. John Adams, a simple farmer's son, gave up a successful law practice at thirty-nine to enter the Continental Congress, and after that, with very minor exceptions, he had no private employment for the remaining fifty-two years of his life. His son John Quincy Adams, from his admission to the bar in his early twenties until his death at eighty-one, was outside government service for just seven years. During their combined appointive and elective careers of seventy-eight years, they received little in the way of monetary satisfaction from a young nation that prided itself on meager public salaries. "A curiosity" was what John Adams called the $5,000 he annually received for being vice president of the United States; as secretary of state, John Quincy Adams was paid $3,500 a year.[13]

The plight of the first two generations of Adamses was further complicated by the nature of the offices they held. As representatives of the United States in the diplomatic community, they were expected to live and entertain at expense levels well above their government remunerations. Adams figured that while he was secretary of state, his expenses exceeded his salary by $4,000 to $5,000 a year. They were poor men playing in a rich man's league. John Quincy Adams's salary while he was minister to Russia was second only to that of the president of the United States. Yet it was a paltry figure when compared to the $350,000 a year that the French government gave its ambassador for official expenses.[14] The immensely practical Abigail Adams was so worried about her son's financial position that she asked President Madison to recall him from Russia. Madison obliged, and even offered the young man a seat on the Supreme Court, which the Senate confirmed. But he declined the honor. The Adams men would always grumble and do their duty.

It was not until the death of Peter Chardon Brooks in 1849 that the Adams family was on firm financial footing. Brooks was the father-in-law of Charles Francis Adams, and Boston's first millionaire. His estate settled $300,000 on the third-generation Adamses. The generous bequest may have turned out to be a double-edged sword that contributed to the decline of the dynasty. For in the fourth generation the financially independent Brooks Adams would write to his financially independent brother Henry,

"The greatest relief a man can have is a fixed occupation, which has become a second nature, and which absorbs his time. Our misfortune has been that this necessary application of our energy has been denied us. We live largely on ourselves."[15]

DESPITE HAVING POLITICALLY UNPALATABLE personalities, which all the Adamses vigorously contended could not be altered, a collection of formidable enemies, and a lack of financial means, the Adamses built a great political dynasty. They succeeded, against mountainous odds, by sheer intellectual ability and an inherited capacity for hard work.

During his years in the Continental Congress, John Adams served on more than ninety committees and was chairman of twenty-five; his son John Quincy Adams was still working a twelve-, thirteen-, and even eighteen-hour day at seventy years of age. Nothing pleased John Adams more than when a Baltimore newspaper called him an "old fielder"—for, as he explained to Abigail, "An old fielder is a tough, hardy, laborious little horse that works very hard and lives upon very little."[16]

The Adamses established unsurpassed records for industry in every job they held. After his four colleagues left Ghent, John Quincy Adams stayed on to complete the record of the negotiations that ended the War of 1812, although it meant that his wife and seven-year-old son had to travel alone across 2,000 miles of war-torn Europe in midwinter. Later, when he was secretary of state, Congress assigned him the task of preparing a report on weights and measures. This was the type of job that is traditionally sloughed off on subordinates. But not by Secretary Adams. He spent three years of his spare time writing a weighty tome that has become a scientific classic. John Quincy Adams also achieved the dubious distinction of being probably the only American foreign minister to have been locked in the State Department offices by a janitor while working long after the official closing hour.

This energy was a manifestation of the Adams ambition and willpower. John Adams wrote to his son, a twenty-seven-year-old lawyer, "If you do not rise to the head not only of your profession but of your country, it will be owing to your own laziness, slovenliness, and obstinacy."[17] It has been said that only five presidents dreamed from boyhood of being in the White House, but this was the dream of almost every male Adams for three generations. John Quincy rose to be the head of his country, as his father had predicted; Charles Francis ran for vice president and narrowly missed a presidential nomination; John Quincy II also ran for vice president; Brooks Adams waited in vain for the vice presidential nomination at the 1896 Democratic Convention; even Henry Adams, now remembered for his other-worldliness, had great if ill-defined ambitions during his early career. As a fledgling reporter he talked of making his political writing into "a power in the land," and while disclaiming ambition for political office, Henry added, "*except very high office* I would take none."[18]

Yet it was a strict Adams rule, only rarely broken, not to lift a finger to aid one's own political ambition. A frustrated supporter, waiting for John Quincy Adams to declare himself for the presidency in 1824, wrote his reluctant favorite, "Kings are made by politicians and newspapers; and the man who sits down waiting to be crowned either by chance or just right will go bare-headed all his life."[19] The Adams doctrine of "the office seeks the man" was carried to its ultimate application in 1833 when John Quincy was a candidate for governor of Massachusetts and his son Charles Francis was running for the state legislature: the younger Adams voted for neither his father nor himself!

WHILE THESE INDUSTRIOUS, INTELLECTUAL Adamses were building a massive record of achievement, there were others in the family who fared less well. It was almost unconscionably difficult to be an Adams, and not all who were so blessed could live up to their inheritance. As Henry Cabot Lodge Sr. said, "This remarkable heritage brought to those who received it burdens as well as honor."[20] As often as not, the burdens exceeded the honor.

Of the three sons of Abigail and John Adams, one became president of the United States, but the lives of two dissolved in drink. Their daughter lived an equally unhappy life, although not of her own volition. John Quincy Adams also had three sons: one committed suicide in his late twenties and another died in his early thirties, which left Charles Francis, as he wrote in his diary, "the only one who remains to keep the name and the family in our branch at least from destruction."[21]

On the last day of 1798, President John Adams wrote his wife, "My children give me more pain than all my enemies."[22] His daughter and first-born, Abigail, had married Colonel William Stephens Smith when her father was minister to Great Britain and Smith was secretary to the legation. The tall, dark, and dashing officer, a former aide-de-camp to General Washington, was to spend the remainder of his years in pursuit of pleasures that he could not afford, in pursuit of land speculations that rarely materialized, and in pursuit of public sinecures, which were supplied by his father-in-law at considerable moral and political cost. (Ironically, the very odd young man whom John Adams's daughter jilted went on to become a famous playwright and chief justice of the Vermont Supreme Court.)[23]

The son for whom President John Adams grieved was Charles, three years younger than John Quincy. During the Revolution the father had taken the two boys with him to Europe, but while John Quincy went on to Russia as private secretary to the American diplomat Francis Dana, Charles became homesick and returned to his mother in Massachusetts. After Harvard and a legal training he married Sally Smith, the sister of William Stephens Smith, a "modest and composed" girl, in the opinion of her mother-in-law. Charles was to give the Smith family as much grief as his brother-in-law was to give the Adamses. He too was affected by the get-rich-quick lures of land speculation, and his ruinous losses were compounded by the guilt of having also lost the savings that John Quincy had entrusted to his care. Charles became an alcoholic and died at thirty. The father received the news at almost the same moment that he learned of his loss of the presidency to Jefferson.

John Adams's other unfortunate son was Thomas Boylston, the youngest child, who lived with his father in the ex-president's last years. Thomas also drank too much, and periodically deserted his family. His nephew Charles Francis, then at Harvard, unctuously decided that Thomas's fate "was necessary to check our pride."[24]

Most tragic was the fate of John Quincy's eldest child, George Washington Adams. When he was born in Berlin in 1801, the young father wrote, "I know not whether upon rigorous philosophical principles it is wise to give a great and venerable name to such a lottery-ticket as a new-born infant— but my logical scruples have in this case been overpowered by my instinctive sentiments."[25] George turned out to be a brilliant young man who beat Ralph Waldo Emerson in competition for the Boylston Prize at Harvard, studied law with Daniel Webster, and was elected to the Massachusetts legislature at twenty-five. Yet he was erratic, undisciplined, and irresponsible. Filled with his private romantic dreams, he left his personal and business affairs in a tatter. The Puritan sermons of his well-meaning and devoted father only added to his inability to cope with reality. Even in his dreams he heard his father admonishing, "Remember, George, who you are, what you are doing!"[26]

The Adams Dynasty—*A Selective Genealogy*

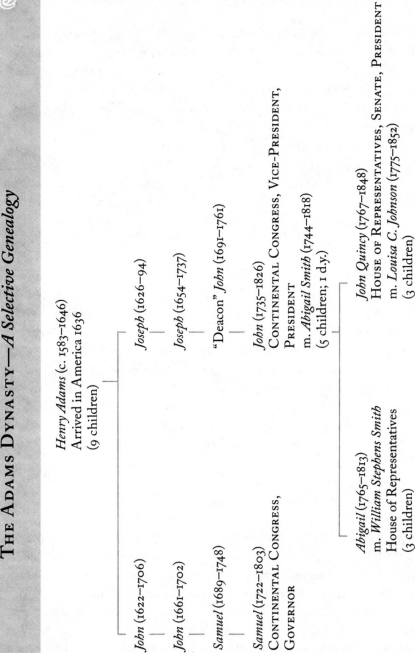

Henry Adams (c. 1583–1646)
Arrived in America 1636
(9 children)

Joseph (1626–94)

Joseph (1654–1737)

"Deacon" John (1691–1761)

John (1735–1826)
Continental Congress, Vice-President,
President
m. *Abigail Smith* (1744–1818)
(5 children; 1 d.y.)

John (1622–1706)

John (1661–1702)

Samuel (1689–1748)

Samuel (1722–1803)
Continental Congress,
Governor

Abigail (1765–1813)
m. *William Stephens Smith*
House of Representatives
(3 children)

John Quincy (1767–1848)
House of Representatives, Senate, President
m. *Louisa C. Johnson* (1775–1852)
(3 children)

George Washington (1801–28)
(unmarried)

Charles Francis (1807–86)
HOUSE OF REPRESENTATIVES,
minister to Great Britain
m. Abigail Brooks (1808–1889)
(6 children; 1 d.y.)

Brooks (1848–1927)
Author
m. Evelyn Davis (1835–1926)
(no issue)

Henry (1838–1918)
Author
m. Marian Hooper (1843–85)
(no issue)

Charles Francis (1835–1915)
Author, RAILROAD president
m. Mary Ogden (1843–1935)
(5 children)

John Quincy (1883–94)
Democratic leader of Massachusetts
m. Fanny Crowninshield
(1834–1911)
(6 children; 2 d.y.)

Charles Francis (1866–1954)
Secretary of Navy
m. Frances Lovering (1869–1956)
(2 children)

Catherine (1902–1988)
m. Henry Sturgis Morgan
(5 children)

Charles Francis (1910–1999)
Business Executive
m. Margaret Stockton
(3 children)

On April 29, 1828, George took a steamboat to Washington. The engines kept telling him, "Let it be, let it be, let it be, let it be." In the middle of the night he awakened a passenger to ask if the stranger had been spreading rumors against him. He asked the captain to stop the ship and put him ashore because "there is a combination among the passengers against me." The hallucinatory young man added, "I heard them talking and laughing at me."[27] In the morning George's hat was found on the upper deck; the former president claimed his son's body at the New York morgue.

George had left a note for his brother, asking him to look after a young girl he had made pregnant. Charles Francis destroyed the letter. "I shall do what I can in pursuit of the spirit of the request, though I confess the whole to be a foolish effusion of a thoughtless moment," wrote the brother in his diary.[28]

FROM 1636, WHEN HENRY Adams brought his nine children to Massachusetts from England, until the birth of Samuel Adams in 1722, the most exalted Adams was a village pastor in New Hampshire. The records of these early Adamses, according to the second Adams to be president of the United States, were "of humble life, but there is nothing in them of which a descendant need be ashamed."[29] They were typical New England yeomen. John Adams, known as "the Deacon," the father of the first Adams president, was a farmer, cordwainer or shoemaker, tithingman, and village selectman.

Then suddenly, without explanation, this line of uninterrupted mediocrity was shattered by two signers of the Declaration of Independence.

Samuel and John Adams were second cousins; Sam, the elder by thirteen years, tutored his young relation in revolution. And "this brace of Adamses," as they were called by old Governor Shirley, teamed up with the Lees of Virginia to maneuver the separation from Great Britain. It was inevitable that peace would separate the cousins politically. As John wrote his wife, "Master Cleverly used to say thirty years ago, 'I pity Mr. Sam Adams, for he was born a rebel.'" John added, "I hope he will not die one."[30] But Sam, the greatest manager of the mob in American history, had little talent for constructive statesmanship and died a hard-shelled reactionary. Moreover, he had only daughters, and so the political dynasty would be carried forward through his cousin's line.

Deacon John Adams left the bulk of his estate to his sons Elihu and Peter Boylston. Elihu became a militia captain and died of dysentery early in the Revolution; Peter lived a long life as a Quincy farmer in the manner of his father. The eldest son, John Adams, received the greatest inheritance, an education.

After college and a brief try at teaching, he turned to the law. And while a struggling young lawyer he married Abigail, daughter of the Reverend William Smith. The marriage was objected to by Mrs. Smith, who was a Quincy, and whose father, the Honorable John Quincy, had been Speaker of the Massachusetts House of Representatives for fourteen years. Mrs. Smith's daughter deserved better than the son of Deacon John Adams.

The union of Abigail Smith and John Adams was a long and constant love affair. Thirty-one years later Abigail would write her husband, "Years subdue the ardor of passion, but in lieu thereof a friendship and affection, deep rooted, subsists which defies the ravages of time, and will survive whilst the flame exists. Our attachments . . . increase, I believe, with our years."[31]

She was more than a lover and the bearer of John's five children, one of whom died in infancy. For she had the "capacity to comprehend." Their letters are a blend of love *and* politics; and hers, as John admitted, "are much better worth preserving than mine." Her graceful comments and apt quotations were even raided by her husband for his own use in corresponding with the leaders of the nation. In truth, John Adams called his wife "My best, my dearest, my wisest friend in this world."[32]

Their marriage was marked by long separations. After thirteen years as Mrs. John Adams, Abigail wrote that "not more than half that time have we had the happiness of living together."[33] And the years apart increased as her husband served his country in congresses and diplomatic posts. While John worked at revolution, Abigail was their children's protector, teacher, disciplinarian, and even breadwinner. Taxes and inflation were high during the war, and as the demand for farmworkers increased the cost of labor, Abigail's response was to reorganize the farm and bring in tenants to split the harvest with her fifty-fifty. At the same time, she went into trade. At first, John in France sent her small packets of goods, such as handkerchiefs (one shipment delivered by Lafayette!), which she arranged with a merchant to sell. John favored this "small is best" system, fearing loss from enemy frigates. Abigail explained that this was buying at high retail prices when she could do better wholesale with larger orders. Don't worry, she wrote. "If one in 3 arrives I should be a gainer." Moreover, her system could factor in consumer taste and the demands of the market. At one point linen was "in great demand"; ten weeks later it was "well supplied." John concluded that her business sense was superior to his and gladly left commerce to his wife.[34]

JOHN ADAMS CAME MORE slowly to a belief in American independence than his cousin Sam. He was first concerned with justice. (He and his heirs would always be first concerned with abstracts; they were more comfortable with generalities than with particulars.) In 1770 John Adams's abstract justice led him to defend the British captain Thomas Preston and his soldiers when they were tried for firing on the citizens of Boston. He knew the "Boston Massacre" had been incited; the mob was wrong. It was a made-to-order cause for Adams, who enjoyed playing the martyr and now felt he was sacrificing his political future. But Sam Adams could not afford his cousin's self-righteousness: independence was an end that necessitated some unholy means. John won his case and, quickly thereafter, a seat in the Massachusetts legislature as well.

When he was elected to the Continental Congress in 1774, John was a provincial lawyer who had only once been outside his own colony. Three years before he had gone to Connecticut to take a mineral water cure. (Hypochondria was another Adams trait, though they quickly forgot their ailments when involved in a cause.) And so he rode off to Philadelphia to "see a little more of the world" and to enter "the theater of action."

The Puritan found Philadelphia to be a city of "sinful feasts" of "everything which could delight the eye or allure the taste; curds and creams, jellies, sweetmeats of various sorts, twenty sorts of tarts, fools, trifles, floating islands, whipped syllabubs . . . Parmesan cheese, punch, wine, porter, beer, etc."[35] For a man who would not allow his wife to read Lord Chesterfield's letters because they were "stained with libertine morals," it was a rude shock to find that he enjoyed these new sensations. It was the beginning of a lifelong struggle, wrote biographer Page Smith, "in which the hedonist had as ally Adams' passionate involvement in life, and the Puritan a conscience hammered out by four generations of forebears who had carried on an unending dialogue with God."[36]

"This assembly is like no other that ever existed," Adams wrote from Philadelphia. "Every man in it is a great man, an orator, a critic, a statesman; and therefore every man upon every question must show his oratory, his criticism, and his political abilities. The consequence of this is that business is drawn and spun out to an immeasurable length. I believe if it was moved and seconded that three and two make five, we should be entertained with logic and rhetoric, law, history, politics, and mathematics, and then—we should pass the resolution unanimously in the affirmative."[37] Yet during the long and tedious sessions Adams proposed George Washington as commander in chief, a masterful stroke of continental unity; he almost single-handedly founded the American navy; and, as chairman of the Board of War and Ordnance, he began to build America's war machine. But the crowning achievement of his four years in the Congress was independence. Wrote Richard Stockton, a delegate from New Jersey, "I call him the Atlas of American independence. He it was who sustained the debate, and by the force of his reasoning demonstrated not only the justice but the expediency of the measure."[38]

In November 1777, Congress elected Adams to a three-man commission to France. The next February he left America with his eleven-year-old son John Quincy. And with the exception of four months in 1779, he remained abroad for a decade, for nearly six years without his wife.

His diplomatic career was checkered. Abigail proudly said that her husband was "made of the oak instead of the willow. He may be torn up by the roots, or break, but he will never bend."[39] This was hardly the stuff of which successful diplomats are made. On the ornamental level, a friend lamented of Adams, "He can't dance, drink, game, flatter, promise, dress, swear with the gentlemen, and small talk and flirt with the ladies—in short, he has none of the essential *arts* and *ornaments* which make a courtier."[40] And yet, unable to swim in the social whirl and unwilling to bend when principle was involved, John Adams participated in two amazing diplomatic accomplishments, one of which was solely on his own responsibility.

France was America's greatest ally. But, under Louis XVI and Foreign Minister Vergennes, it was also an absolute monarchy playing the time-honored game of balancing alliances for its own protection and advancement. The North American revolution was a useful piece to manipulate on the board of world power. Benjamin Franklin, the senior American diplomat, understood this game; he would move in his country's best interests when the circumstances were right. Arthur Lee, the other commissioner in France, was a patriotic zealot, unwilling to play by these rules. By temperament and training, John Adams was to side with Lee, as he had sided with Lee's brothers in the Continental Congress. His presence in France only compromised the delicate American position. Fortunately, he realized that the tripartite American mission was unworkable and recommended to Congress a single representative, which by experience and prestige would have to be Franklin. Ten months after his arrival in Paris he was on his way home. His first mission abroad was a failure.

The three months that were allotted to Adams in America before he returned to Europe were spent in more productive pursuits. On his arrival in Massachusetts in August 1779 he was elected to a state convention to draft a constitution. This was an ideal assignment; nothing pleased an Adams so much as considering general principles of government. John Adams wrote the document, which became the model for the constitutions of other states and would influence the writing of the federal Constitution. The Adams constitution was built on "balanced" government: a two-house legislature, a strong executive, and an independent judiciary.

Adams then returned to Europe to negotiate treaties of peace and commerce with Great Britain at such time as the mother country might be ready to consider them. The thought of the unbending Bostonian as sole negotiator was not an especially pleasing one to Vergennes. So the French minister, working behind Adams's back, managed to get Congress to broaden the peace commission to five members. Adams was to be joined by Franklin, Jay, Jefferson, and Henry Laurens of South Carolina. The question now for Adams was what to do with his time until Britain was prepared to negotiate. Franklin typically suggested that he should relax and enjoy the pleasures of France—an idea that Adams was incapable of considering. It was at this point that Adams, acting without congressional mandate, went to Holland to see about a loan to relieve the serious financial pressures on his war-torn country. By the time he left Europe in 1788 he had successfully concluded four Dutch loans, thus saving the credit of the United States.

His second diplomatic triumph, in collaboration with his able colleagues, was the treaty of peace with Great Britain. The Americans were not in a strong bargaining position. The war had exhausted the insurgent nation and could not have been continued indefinitely. Yet the American negotiators received far more than they conceded, Adams's particular contribution being the securing of the Newfoundland fishery rights.

Now, after their long separation, Abigail and her daughter joined him in Europe, and John Quincy Adams made an important decision. The son had been eleven when Adams went to France. He was now eighteen. During the years abroad he had studied at a private school in France and at the University of Leyden, had spent two years in St. Petersburg as private secretary to the American representative to Russia, and had served as his father's secretary in Holland and during the peace negotiations in Paris. He read or spoke Greek, Latin, Dutch, French, and German. He had listened to and questioned the great men of the world. The temptation to remain in Europe was great, but he was determined to return home and become a schoolboy again. (Perhaps the example of William Temple Franklin influenced him: Benjamin Franklin's grandson also went to France as a boy, and had turned into a dandy who could be seen leading a cat around by a ribbon.) So in 1785 John Quincy Adams sailed for Boston and Harvard.

It was to be the fate of successive generations of Adamses to serve their country in London during the three most strained periods of Anglo-American relations: after the War for Independence, after the War of 1812, and during the Civil War. In the year that John Quincy entered Harvard, his father was appointed the first minister to Great Britain. There was a dramatic confrontation between the stocky ex-rebel and his former king. Had circumstances been different, John Adams might have stood before George III as a traitor in irons rather than as the accredited representative of the United States of America. Despite a chilly reception from British society and an inability to adapt to life at court, Adams's dogged determination and intense patriotism brought him diplomatic success.

In 1788 John Adams sailed for home and the third phase of an amazing career. As a legislator, he had helped achieve the colonies' independence; as a diplomat, he had helped secure it. Now, as an executive, he would see if he could make it work.

But before entering the White House he was to spend eight unhappy years as the vice president of the United States. It took unbearable self-control to be the silent presiding officer of the Senate—self-control that he did not always possess. He bitterly complained, "My country has in its wisdom contrived for me the most insignificant office that was the invention of man."[41]

SPEAKING WITH OBVIOUS PRIDE and excitement, Vice President Adams in 1794 announced to the Senate that George Washington had nominated his son to be minister resident to the Netherlands. The appointment of John Quincy Adams had been Washington's idea; the vice president had discreetly resisted pressuring his superior. Yet young Adams, with his knowledge of Holland and its language, was a natural choice. Besides, it was a most insignificant legation.

Once John Quincy Adams had been his father's diplomatic secretary; now he took his brother Thomas with him. This form of apprenticeship was to be an Adams tradition for three generations and an incomparable experience for the younger members of the family.[42] (With one exception, all the young assistants performed with credit.)

Because of the wars of the French Revolution, the U.S. embassy in The Hague was to become America's most important listening post in Europe, and the twenty-seven-year-old minister was to live up to the expectations of President Washington, who wrote the young man's proud father, "I shall be much mistaken if, in as short a period as can well be expected, he is not found at the head of the diplomatic corps."[43] Some, however, were not so pleased by the prospects of an Adams dynasty. On the eve of the 1796 presidential election Samuel Harrison Smith's Philadelphia *New World* urged readers to vote for Jefferson because "Adams has sons who might aim to succeed their father; Jefferson, like Washington, has no son."[44]

The question of nepotism also troubled the Adamses. John Quincy was much opposed to accepting an appointment from his father. After John became president, his son wrote Abigail, "Louis the 14th was one day expressing his astonishment at the stupidity of a certain ambassador at his court. 'He must be the relative of some minister.'" John Quincy added, "I have no desire to be the application for a similar reflection." Washington, however, urged his successor to keep John Quincy in the diplomatic corps because he "is the most valuable public character we have abroad," and the new president then named his son to be minister plenipotentiary to Prussia. "Merit in my family," he wrote John Quincy, "deserves as much of its Country as in another."[45] The decision was a relatively easy one. His son was a diplomat of obvious worth, and, in an administration noted for disloyalty to its chief executive, Adams was at least assured of direct and reliable reporting from the European scene.[46]

Other relatives and in-laws were not as reliable. During the four White House years, Abigail was often sick. Their son Charles was sinking rapidly and would die before the end of the presidential term. John Quincy had married while overseas, and a federal job had to be found for his bankrupt father-in-law. (He was made director of stamps.) A son of Abigail's sister had also gone bankrupt, and turned to his uncle. (He was made an assistant judge in the District of Columbia.)

And there was the constant embarrassment of son-in-law William Stephens Smith. The president sent his name, along with a list of military appointments, to the Senate to be adjutant general of the army. Smith was the only man rejected. Adams then made him a lieutenant colonel in charge of a provisional regiment. But when the regiment was disbanded, another position had to be found. He was made surveyor of the District of New York and inspector of the revenue. Later Smith was dismissed when he became

Abigail Smith Adams, 1744–1818

involved in a South American revolution. By this time Adams had left office and could no longer help his lovely daughter's improvident husband.

Minor acts of nepotism were politically irritating but hardly the cause of John Adams's fall. With the passing of George Washington, the last dike to hold back the party division was gone. Adams might be the head of the government, but Hamilton was head of his party. And Hamilton and the Federalists wanted war with France. Adams's one great act as president, perhaps the greatest act of his public life, was that he kept the peace. Hamilton and his party would not forgive him this wise course.

The president went into the election of 1800 with a united Jeffersonian party against him and a badly divided Hamiltonian party as his nominal ally. George Cabot, a high priest of federalism, wrote, "We shall do as well with Jefferson for President . . . as with anything we can now expect."[47] Yet Adams ran far ahead of his own party, and a change of 250 votes in New York City would have brought his reelection. Adams felt that the cause of his defeat was his peace mission to France. Abigail's analysis was probably more correct: "The defection of New York has been the source [of defeat]," she wrote. "That defection was produced by the intrigues of two men [Hamilton and Burr]."[48]

John Adams's public life was now ended. He returned to Quincy decidedly land-poor, having put most of his capital, over $50,000, into the purchase of 900 acres. If it had not been for the secret savings of Abigail, invested in securities, the former president might have been in dire distress. He would spend the quarter century still allotted to him as a farmer, prolific letter writer, and enthusiastic observer of his brilliant son's career.

UPON HIS DEFEAT, JOHN Adams immediately recalled his son from Berlin. The returning diplomat brought home a wife and an infant son. In 1797 John Quincy had married Louisa Catherine Johnson, daughter of the American consul in London and a niece of Thomas Johnson, the Revolutionary-era governor of Maryland. Her father had been sent to London by an Annapolis firm before the Revolution, had married a middle-class Englishwoman, and had spent the war years in France.

It was at first unclear to John Quincy's patriotic parents whether their son was contracting a union with an English girl. Abigail wrote her son, "I would hope for the love I bear my country that the Siren is at least *half-blood*." An opposition newspaper in Boston quickly sought to make political capital of the match: "Young John [Quincy] Adams' negotiations have terminated in a marriage with an English lady. . . . It is a happy circumstance that he had made no other Treaty." This misconception would remain a political albatross throughout John Quincy's career. As late as the presidential campaign of 1828, his opponents in western Pennsylvania were passing stories about his "English" wife.[49]

When he brought his wife of four years home on a New England Thanksgiving in 1801, it was like stepping into Noah's Ark for the frail and poetical Louisa. Confronted with the rustic Yankees and her competent mother-in-law, she felt herself "literally and without knowing it a *fine* lady." To her grandson Henry she would be remembered as "an exotic, like her Sevres china." But she "could never be Bostonian, and it was her cross in life."[50]

Louisa was cultivated, retiring, romantic; her husband was an Adams—stiff, combative, restless. During their more than fifty years of marriage she would never feel at home with "the disgusting realities of a heartless political life." The official social calls were a torment. The long separations from her children, she felt, were partly to blame for their tragic lives. She called her attempt at autobiography *The Adventures of a Nobody*. Written during a period of physical ills and emotional stress, it is a pitiable tale, recounting how her father's bankruptcy, only two weeks after her wedding, "gave a colouring to my days, which could never be eradicated . . . [and] turned every sweet into gall."[51] Yet John Quincy never felt that he had been the unsuspecting suitor tricked into marriage by an impoverished family. In his own memoirs, probably more accurate than his wife's, he acknowledges that "our union has not been without its trials" but speaks of Louisa as "a faithful and affectionate wife, and a careful, tender, indulgent, and watchful mother to our children."[52]

The couple was back in Boston scarcely a year when the Massachusetts legislature sent John Quincy to the U.S. Senate. Jefferson, his father's Republican enemy, was president; the freshman legislator had been elected by the Federalists. Yet he promptly approved the president's Louisiana Purchase, earning the enmity of the Federalists, and opposed the administration's plan for governing and taxing the territory, earning the enmity of the Republicans. The incapacity of an Adams to live under party government, begun by his father, was sharpened to an art by the son. In his long career John Quincy would break with every political party that elected him to office. "I have been styled a deserter from all parties because I truly never belonged to any party," he later wrote.[53]

The final break with the Federalists came with his support of the Embargo Act of 1807. It was a just retaliation, in his opinion, for the British firing on American ships and impressment of American sailors. But it was against the pro-British inclinations of his party and the commercial interests of his state. Recalling John Adams's unpopular peace mission to France, the Federalist Theodore Lyman wrote, "Curse on the stripling, how he apes his sire!"[54] John Quincy prophetically predicted that his vote would cost him his Senate seat. Nine months before the end of his term the Massachusetts legislature elected a successor and instructed him to vote for the repeal of the embargo. Adams promptly resigned. (His five years in Washington made little contribution to the national good but a century and a half later earned him a "profile in courage" from another young Bay State senator, John F. Kennedy.)

His next assignment, as minister to Russia, was given him by President Madison, Jefferson's heir. On August 5, 1809, a little over a year after his hasty exit from the Senate, Mr. and Mrs. John Quincy Adams and two-year-old Charles Francis left for the imperial court in St. Petersburg.[55] The Adamses' two eldest sons remained in Quincy under the watchful supervision of their grandparents.

The Russia to which Adams was being sent, in his opinion, "has been thawed out of her eternal snow and has crawled or stalked over all Europe, a tremendous power whose future influence cannot be foreseen."[56] At court, John Quincy got on well with Tsar Alexander, with whom he took morning strolls. But this was still not a diplomatic assignment of the highest magnitude, nor were his five years in Russia of major importance in the shaping of American foreign policy. Yet just as his minor post in Holland had proved to be an excellent vantage point for observing the wars of the French Revolution, so now was Russia proving to be a window on the Napoleonic Wars.[57] John Quincy had the good fortune to be in the right places at the right times.

In 1815 there was another parallel in the astonishingly similar careers of John Adams and John Quincy Adams. Just as the father had been the senior American representative on the commission that negotiated peace with Great Britain in 1783, so now was his son named the senior American representative on the commission to conclude the second treaty of peace with Great Britain. The first American commission had outmaneuvered the British and won a treaty well above the expectations of the situation. The second American commission was equally superior to its counterpart, and secured an equally favorable treaty.[58] The United States had taken a beating in the War of 1812. Even its greatest victory, Jackson's at New Orleans, came too late to be known to the American negotiators. Yet the peace treaty was concluded without the loss of any rights. Again the particular contribution of the Adams negotiator was the protection of the Newfoundland fisheries.

With the successful conclusion of the peace conference, John Quincy, still following in his father's footsteps, was rewarded with the English mission. As the second Adams envoy to Great Britain, he would feel the same cool breeze of society and the same pinch of economy. John Adams warned him, "The corps diplomatique will say 'Adams lives *dans la plus infame oeconomy.*' Their coachmen and footmen will look down on yours with the utmost scorn and contempt. . . . *Quid inde?* Your father has seen and felt all this before you."[59]

John Quincy brought his two eldest sons to London. Charles Francis and John were sent to a boarding school at Ealing, where their lives were complicated by the taunts of their classmates. One English boy asked John if he had ever been at Washington (a sly reference to the burning of the capital by the British troops). "No," replied the patriotic youth, "but I have been at New Orleans."[60] The Adams children would always be fighting their parents' battles. Years later young Henry Adams, son of Charles Francis of the Ealing school, would indignantly see his Boston chums wearing black armbands because of Charles Sumner's election to the Senate, and in defense of his father's abolitionist sentiments would put on a white armband.

The office of secretary of state was considered a stepping-stone to the presidency. Of Washington's successors, only John Adams had not occupied it. In 1817 the new president, James Monroe, himself a former secretary of state, had the choice of three qualified men for the position—Albert Gallatin, Henry Clay, and John Quincy Adams. But the first two had political liabilities, and Adams got the coveted assignment.[61]

Arriving in the United States after eight years abroad, the new secretary of state hurried to his aged parents in Quincy—but first he had to bring his diary up to date—and while journaling, he missed the steamboat to take him to the eagerly awaited reunion!

Henry Adams once wrote that his grandfather "was always on the outskirts,—a kind of free lance, following the march of forces which he never commanded."[62] There was considerable validity in the assessment. John Quincy's presidency was to be a failure. Even his great fight against slavery would be only a preliminary bout. But for eight years as secretary of state he was a major force in molding American history. These were richly productive years: he settled the long-smoldering Florida question, with Spain ceding the territory to the United States; he settled the western boundary of Louisiana; he concluded a treaty with Russia that limited that nation's claims to the Northwest; he was the architect of the Monroe Doctrine, defining U.S. interests in the Western Hemisphere.

Early in his career John Quincy told his father, "I have been accustomed all my life to plain dealing and candor, and am not sufficiently versed in the art of political swindling to be prepared for negotiating with an European Minister of State."[63] Yet as Henry Cabot Lodge Sr. later said, an Adams "judged himself far more severely, far more harshly . . . than any dispassionate critic would think of doing."[64] Because of, or in spite of, his Puritan character, John Quincy Adams ranked among his nation's greatest foreign secretaries.

Now the vastly ambitious Adams was within striking distance of his goal. His one sadness was that his mother had not lived to see him elevated to the White House, in whose bare ballroom she had once hung the family wash. John Quincy had always been extremely close to his mother. Within minutes of signing the Treaty of Ghent he had sent Abigail the important news; three days later he wrote his wife. On October 28, 1818, he told his diary:

Had she lived to the age of the Patriarchs every day of her life would have been filled with clouds of goodness and of love. There is not a virtue that can abide in the female heart but it was an ornament of hers. She had been fifty-four years the delight of my father's heart, the sweetener of all his toils, the comforter of all his sorrows, the sharer and heightener of all his joys. It was but the last time when I saw my father that he told me, with an ejaculation of gratitude to the Giver of every good and perfect gift, that in all the vicissitudes of his fortune, through all the good report and evil report of the world, in all his struggles and in all his sorrows, the affectionate participation and cheering encouragement of his wife had been his never-failing support, without which he was sure he should never have lived through them.[65]

There were four candidates for the presidency in 1824—Andrew Jackson, John Quincy Adams, William H. Crawford, and Henry Clay. None had a majority, and the election would be decided by the House of Representatives from among the top three contenders. Crawford had a stroke, and the contest narrowed to Jackson and Adams. The support of Clay would settle the contest.

Here was Adams, the unbending Puritan, the inheritor of a tradition that the office seeks the man, the candidate who had not aided his own cause during the canvass, now placed in a position where he must bargain to obtain the office that was his life's ambition. This he knew. He wrote, "There is in my prospects and anticipations a solemnity and moment never before experienced, and to which *unaided nature is inadequate*." Bargain he did, though he would not even admit it to his diary. Clay's emissaries came to him and he wrote, "*Incedo super ignes* [I am treading coals of fire]."[66] The House made Adams president, and Adams made Clay his secretary of state. This was a topic for Washington wits. Margaret Bayard Smith reported: Prometheus had made a clay man and the United States now had a "Clay President."[67]

John Quincy told his son, "No person can ever be a thorough partisan for a long period without sacrifice of his moral identity. The skill consists in knowing exactly where to draw the line." John Quincy Adams drew the line *after* the presidency. ("The Puritan character," Henry Adams would write, "could be supple enough when it chose.")[68]

The "deal" that made Adams president was probably unspoken. Clay could never have supported Jackson under any circumstances, and he was also the logical choice for secretary of state. Yet it would haunt and finally defeat Adams. He was a minority president. The vice president and the Congress were against him. He would not use the powers of the chief executive in his own behalf. During four years he removed only twelve persons from office, nor would he appoint his supporters. "The friends of the Administration have to contend not only against their enemies, but against the Administration itself," said Henry Clay, "which leaves its powers in the hands of its own enemies."[69] And on top of this the opposition was given a magnificent rallying cry: the supposed deal between Adams and Clay.

Immediately upon his election, John Quincy Adams notified his father. The old president replied, "My dear Son . . . Never did I feel so much solemnity as upon this occasion. The multitude of my thoughts, and the intensity of my feelings are too much for a mind like mine, in its ninetieth year."[70] The ancient patriot did not live to see the full suffering of his son in the White House. On July 4, 1826, he died at the age of ninety-one. On the same day in Monticello, death came to Thomas Jefferson. It was a remarkable coincidence. On the fiftieth anniversary of the Declaration of Independence, the man who wrote it and the man who secured its passage left this world together.[71] President John Adams was laid to rest in his beloved Quincy, while the pastor read from the first book of Chronicles: "He died in a good old age, full of days, riches, and honor, and Solomon his son reigned in his stead."

The second Adams president had a first-rate design for America. He had worked hard to expand its continental boundaries, and now he wanted to span it with roads and canals. It was an ambitious program for "internal improvements." Yet Congress would have no part of it. Rejecting a systematic plan, the best Congress would do was an occasional purchase of stock in some enterprise, such as the Dismal Swamp Canal Company. John Adams had considered his presidency to be a failure; now his son drew the same conclusion of his: "I fell, and with me fell . . . the system of internal improvement by National means and National Energies. The great object of my Life therefore as applied to the Administration of the Government of the United States, has *failed*."[72]

Adams was overwhelmingly defeated by Jackson. During the nation's first fifty years the two Adamses were the only presidents to be denied a second term.

OUT OF OFFICE, JOHN Quincy Adams faced the serious problem of what to do with the remainder of his life. By 1829 the precedent was well established: ex-presidents were expected to lead sedate and rustic retirements. But John Quincy did not have John Adams's type of original mind, which could happily meditate on the state of nature. He was a combatant who loved combat for combat's sake. The former president understood this, writing in his diary, "More than sixty years of incessant active intercourse with the world has made political movement to me as much a necessary of life as atmospheric air. . . . And thus, while a remnant of physical power is left to me to write and speak, the world will retire from me before I shall retire from the world."[73]

There was an opportunity to run for the House of Representatives from the Old Plymouth district in 1830. Charles Francis was bitterly opposed to the move. At twenty-three, he did not yet understand his father. Ralph Waldo Emerson better knew the chemistry of the elder Adams. "Mr. Adams chose wisely and according to his constitution, when, on leaving the Presidency, he went to Congress," the philosopher wrote in his *Journal*. "He is no literary old gentleman, but a bruiser, and loves the *melee*. {}When they talk about his age and venerableness and nearness to the grave, he knows better, he is like one of those old cardinals, who, as quick as he is chosen Pope, throws away his crutches and his crookedness, and is as straight as a boy. He is an old *rogue* who cannot live on slops, but must have sulphuric acid in his tea."[74]

Moreover, John Quincy Adams needed the $8 a day that a congressman received! He had invested heavily and unwisely in a Washington grist and flour mill. By 1832 he owed $42,000, some of it to his former valet.

As disgusting as politics was to Louisa, she was nevertheless happy to see her husband back in harness. She told her son, "Your father is in high spirits dabbling as usual in public affairs while *fancying he has nothing* to do with them. His mind must be occupied with something, and why not this?"[75]

Congressman John Quincy Adams would soon have a cause to match his high spirits.

His distaste for slavery was inherited from his mother. As far back as the Revolution, Abigail had written, "I wish most sincerely there was not a slave in the province! It always seemed a most iniquitous scheme to me to fight ourselves for what we are robbing the Negroes of, who have as good a right to freedom as we have!"[76] Yet John Quincy's last crusade began not as a fight for abolition but over the constitutional question of free speech and petition. The southern slaveholders and their northern allies made a serious tactical mistake when they joined the issues. In 1836 the House of Repre-

Charles Francis Adams, 1807–1886

sentatives passed the notorious gag rule; by 1840 it had become a standing rule of procedure. The House would receive no abolitionist petitions. If the majority could cut off discussion on slavery, why could it not outlaw debate on any other subject? This was a ready-made issue for an Adams.

For nine years John Quincy tried to present abolitionist petitions to the Congress. For nine years he was shouted down, threatened with assassination, brought before the House for censure, and formally charged by the southern representatives with perjury and treason. Julia Gardiner, later to be the wife of President John Tyler, recalled the scene from her vantage point in the congressional gallery: "Mr. Adams was excessively bald, and as he sat in the middle of the House, with his immense petition rolled around a kind of windlass to sustain it, his excitement was manifest in the flaming redness of his bald head, which acted as a chronometer to his audience."[77] At first the old man stood alone; gradually he gained disciples. At long last he had captured the public imagination. He was now "the Old Man Eloquent." And on December 3, 1845, the gag rule was rescinded. John Quincy Adams, seventy-eight years of age, had won his greatest fight.

During these turbulent years Charles Francis Adams, the rather priggish boy, had become a married man. His wife, Abigail Brooks, was the least exceptional of the Adams women, yet proved to be an understanding and successful wife and mother. She was very Victorian; in fact, in her later years she bore a striking resemblance to the English queen. While Adams at first found her temper to be "high," her education "faulty," and her speech at times "unmeaning and loud nonsense," after ten years of marriage he told himself, "Perhaps of all my good fortune . . . the circumstance of my marriage was the greatest incident; For it stimulated me in the right direction and prevented the preponderance of my constitutional shyness and indolence. Of my wife I need not speak as the passage of time has only contributed to make me prize her more highly."[78] The advantages of marriage also included a wealthy father-in-law, Peter Chardon Brooks. Coming from an almost destitute minister's family, Brooks had built a fortune, reputedly $4 million, as a marine insurance broker and used it generously to promote the ambitions of his two political sons-in-law, Adams and Massachusetts governor Edward Everett.

The raising of a family and the deaths of his brothers helped to mature Charles Francis. John Quincy had once written his eldest child, "My sons have not only their own honor but that of two preceding generations to sustain." Charles Francis now carried this burden alone. He recorded in his diary, "Evening, A long conversation with my father. Family pride. A strong instance in himself, much exceeding even what I suspected. I feel at times depressed by it, for now the dependence upon me is perfectly prominent."[79]

He was elected to the Massachusetts House of Representatives in 1840. After three years he was elevated to the state Senate. These five legislative years were important in his development and in his understanding of his father. His slumbering Puritanism suddenly awoke. He became a passionate supporter of his father's fight against the gag rule and an antislavery leader in his own right.

John Quincy Adams now could die at peace, for his great battle had been won and his only living son had at last picked up the mantle of leadership. The Adams dynasty would continue. The old man wrote to his heir:

> I have noticed with inexpressible pleasure your firm unwavering adherence to honest principle, and feeling as I do that my own career of exertion for the cause of my country and of human liberty, is at its close, at the approach of the most portentous crisis that it ever encountered, it is a consolation to me that you have engaged in it, with all your faculties, and such is my faith in the Justice and Mercy of God, that I will die in humble hope, that however severe your trial

may be, your strength will be found equal to it, and will finally result in the glorious triumph of Freedom and of Truth.[80]

The ancient congressman took his seat as usual in the House of Representatives on February 21, 1848. Suddenly he slumped to the floor. He was taken to the Speaker's office, and two days later he died in the Capitol of the United States. John Quincy Adams's last words were, "This is the end of Earth, but I am composed."[81]

The year 1848 was significant in the annals of the Adams dynasty. The second generation passed on; the third generation moved onto the national scene for the first time, and the last member of the fourth generation entered the world.

The Free Soil Party, the new antislavery coalition, met in Buffalo to pick its candidates for the presidential election. In mourning for his father, Charles Francis Adams was wearing a black crepe band on his white hat. This symbolic link to the late antislavery champion did not escape the assembly. The delegates chose Martin Van Buren for president and Charles Francis Adams for vice president. The rallying cry would be "Van Buren and Free Soil; Adams and Liberty."

Each Adams fervently prayed to be allowed by the public to stand or fall on his own worth. Yet each Adams, in his own mind as well as the people's, was so inextricably interwoven with his ancestors that it became increasingly difficult for public and Adams to separate them. Such was the dilemma of Charles Francis Adams. Nowhere in his public career is this inheritance more perplexing than in the 1848 campaign. Charles Francis fully recognized that his nomination was in large part a tribute to the memory of John Quincy Adams. Still, he complained that "the apparent distinction of my name and family has been the thing most in my way."[82] A son would write of him:

> Never claiming anything, or even seeking recognition, because of his father and his grandfather, constant reference to them in connection with himself annoyed, and at times irritated him. He could not habituate himself to it, nor learn to take it lightly and as a matter of course. . . . To have one's ancestors unceasingly flung in one's face is unpleasant, and listening to the charges incessantly rung upon them becomes indubitably monotonous. This, however, all through life, was to an unusual degree the fate of Mr. Adams, and never so much as in the campaign of 1848.[83]

Yet he stood before the Worcester Free Soil Convention, with his striking resemblance to his forebears, and grossly exploited the words of John Adams. "Sink or Swim, Live or Die, Survive or Perish, to go with the liberties of my country, is my fixed determination"—his grandfather had said when he signed the Declaration of Independence—and now he parroted this heritage for dramatic effect. To one observer, it was "as if old John Adams had stepped down from Trumbull's picture . . . to give his benediction."[84]

The Free Soil ticket received almost 300,000 votes, one-tenth of the total ballots cast. General Zachary Taylor was elected president. The antislavery movement went into a decline until the Kansas-Nebraska Act and the formation of the Republican Party.

Charles Francis used his politically enforced leisure to compile *The Works of John Adams* in ten volumes. The time had come to start defending the reputation of the ancestors. Charles Francis, the politician-antiquarian, balanced between past and present; by the end of his sons' generation, the family balance would be almost totally tipped toward the past.

With the revival of antislavery sentiment, a decade after the Free Soil Party's defeat, Republican candidate Charles Francis Adams was elected to Congress from his father's old district. Henry Adams, like Charles Francis before him, disapproved of his father's election. In 1860 Congressman Adams was reelected over Leverett Saltonstall, a Constitutional Union leader, and young Henry, in the Adams tradition, went to Washington as his father's secretary.

It was the "Great Secession Winter" (Henry Adams's term) of 1860–61. As the southern states dropped out of the Union, the big question was which would come first—Lincoln's inauguration or war. It was imperative to the North that the president-elect take over the reins of the federal government. That he did was in part because of the efforts of Senator William Seward and Congressman Charles Francis Adams. Adams, the driving force behind the Committee of Thirty-Three, was determined to keep the Congress talking until Lincoln arrived in the capital. Representative Reuben Davis of Mississippi accurately called Adams's committee "a tub thrown out to the whale, to amuse only, until the 4th of March next."[85] Young Henry Adams listened to his father and Seward plot and maneuver. It was reminiscent of his father's awe at overhearing conversations between John Quincy Adams and Henry Clay, or his grandfather's boyhood recollections of listening to John Adams and Thomas Jefferson. For three generations the Adams children eavesdropped on greatness.

On March 4, Lincoln became president. March 5: Seward became secretary of state. On March 20, Adams was commissioned minister to Great Britain. Yet Charles Francis did not sail for England until the first of May, after Fort Sumter had been attacked. John Quincy Adams II was to be married in April to Fanny Crowninshield of Boston, and his parents wished to attend the ceremony. The Confederate envoys, without equally pressing social obligations, beat Adams to London. By the time the American minister arrived, the British government had issued a proclamation of neutrality. For the first time in more than a century an Adams had thought of family before country; the consequence was a serious diplomatic blow.

But once in London, the third Adams to be U.S. minister to Great Britain made few errors. The English were cold and reserved as usual. But Charles Francis, in the words of a son, "was a little colder and a little more reserved." He beat the British at their own game "for the very good reason that the game was natural to him."[86] And when the British seized the Laird rams, which were being built in Liverpool for the Confederate navy, Adams scored a major diplomatic coup. The Union victories at Gettysburg and Vicksburg combined had depressed the price of Confederate bonds on the European market by thirteen points; the seizure of the deadly warships dropped the price by fourteen points.

During Charles Francis Adams's long tenure in England his eldest son began a career in politics. John Quincy Adams II, the political heir of the fourth generation, moved onto the national scene in August 1866 as a delegate to the National Union Convention. He went to Philadelphia to protest the harsh reconstruction policy of the Radical Republicans. This initial act of defiance sealed his political fate: when he was nominated to be collector of customs at Boston the next year, the Republican Senate rejected his name. Adamses had always been mavericks; now the day of the maverick had passed. John Quincy II promptly became a Democrat, which meant that politically, he no longer expected his reward in this world. At the 1868 Democratic Convention he received one vote for president. Old John Quincy would have been proud of his namesake, and, had that antislavery firebrand had a sense of humor, he would have been amused that the vote had been cast by a South Carolinian.

THE DYNASTY'S LAST CHANCE for a serious presidential nomination came at the 1872 Liberal Republican Convention. Charles Francis Adams was the front runner. But "the Greatest Iceberg" of the Northern Hemisphere did nothing to cultivate the delegates, and actually wrote a letter that had rather the reverse effect. On the first ballot he received 203 votes to 147 for Horace Greeley. On the sixth ballot the publisher was nominated. He was then endorsed by the Democrats, but not before John Quincy Adams II had bolted the convention over the currency question. The Republicans, seeking to take advantage of the split in the opposition ranks, set up a "Straight-Out" Democratic Party, whose convention nominated young Adams for vice president. He immediately declined the "honor," which didn't discourage the decoy party from going ahead with its canvass. John Quincy II thus became the fourth of his dynasty to be on a ticket for national office. The unwilling candidate with the illustrious name received nearly 30,000 votes.

The news of his defeat for the presidential nomination was relayed to Charles Francis Adams while he was on his way to Geneva. His appointment as U.S. representative at the five-nation *Alabama* claims conference was a bitter pill to President Grant but had been insisted on by Secretary of State Hamilton Fish. The British had failed to prevent the Confederacy from building the *Alabama*. Its guns had taken a considerable toll. The British agreed to arbitrate the question of reparations. Only Charles Francis's skill kept the commission from foundering, and the United States was awarded $15,500,000.

This closed the public career of Charles Francis Adams. He had said, "Public life was a very fascinating occupation, but like drinking brandy. The more you indulge in it, the more uncomfortable it leaves you when you stop."[87] The heady brew was never offered again, although his name kept cropping up as a potential candidate for one office or another. In 1875, when he was proposed for the governorship of Massachusetts, Hamilton Fish wrote that it was the "annually returning periodical demand for a pure, an exemplary statesman in the person of Charles Francis Adams—Governor, President—Town Clerk or something."[88]

Returning to the family archives, Charles Francis published a twelve-volume edition of his father's diaries. (He had earlier edited the letters of his grandmother, two volumes of John Adams's letters to Abigail, and the ten-volume *Works of John Adams*.) This herculean task completed, he said, "My mission is ended, and I may rest."[89] He then sank into a mental decline and finally died in 1886, aged seventy-nine.

Each of his sons had a different appraisal of Charles Francis Adams. Brooks, the youngest, wrote, "My father impressed himself upon me as the most remarkable man I have ever known."[90] Charles Francis Jr. in his autobiography wrote of him with barely disguised hatred. About the only good thing he could say was that his father hadn't forced him to go to a public school![91] Henry, the closest to his father, probably had the most unclouded judgment:

> Charles Francis Adams was singular for mental poise—absence of self-assertion or self-consciousness—the faculty of standing apart without seeming aware that he was alone—a balance of mind and temper that neither challenged nor avoided notice, nor admitted question of superiority or inferiority, of jealousy, of personal motives, from any source, even under great pressure. This unusual poise of judgment and temper ripened by age, became the more striking to his son Henry as he learned to measure the mental faculties themselves, which were in no way exceptional either for depth or range. Charles Francis Adams's memory was hardly above the average; his mind was not bold like his grandfather's or restless like his father's, or imaginative or oratorical—still less mathematical; but it worked with singular perfection, admirable self-restraint, and instinctive mastery of form. Within its range it was a model.[92]

The Adams dynasty had flourished for over a century: from John Adams to John Quincy Adams to Charles Francis Adams. A fourth generation now reached maturity, and Mrs. James A. Garfield, while visiting at Quincy in 1869, marveled at their prospects. They "are showing even more marked ability" than their ancestors, she observed.[93] Indeed, in the late 1860s and early 1870s the intellectual and reform circles in America seemed to be ablaze with young Adamses. John Quincy II was rebuilding the discredited Democratic Party, Charles Francis Jr. was exposing the manipulations of the railroad barons, and Henry was shooting off sparks in every direction as a crusading journalist. Yet buried within the brilliance of this youthful foliage was the seed of dynastic destruction.

First of all, the eldest, John Quincy II, recognized by the family as the political heir apparent, was a most unlikely Adams. He was initially suspect as the only member of the dynasty ever to have been accused of having been "a good fellow."[94] Moreover, he didn't even preserve his letters, considering it a "vile family habit."[95] In short, he was everything an Adams was not supposed to be—easygoing, charming, a wit, inclined to indolence, discouraged by strong opposition. After having been twice burned by his opposition to Radical Republicanism and the Grant presidency, he seemed happier fishing and sailing. He once even forgot to appear before the Massachusetts Supreme Court, when he was counsel in an important case, because "the smelts are biting like thunder."[96]

In 1868 he ran as a Democrat for governor of Massachusetts. Unlike his grandfather, he was destined to be in the wrong place at the wrong time. Losing the governorship was to be his lifetime avocation. But he really preferred being moderator of the Quincy town meeting. As his brother Henry pointed out, "He had all he wanted; wealth, children, society, consideration."[97] It was not until the Democrats returned to office in 1892 that he might have also had political power. Grover Cleveland, the first of his party to have been elected president in thirty-two years, tried to persuade John Quincy to enter his cabinet as secretary of the navy. This would have been a fitting tribute to a man who had cheerfully sought political oblivion in the perennial minority party and whose great-grandfather had founded the American navy. But he was in ill health and declined the appointment. Defying family tradition to the end, he died at sixty, considerably short of the fourscore years that are allotted to every Adams.

The fatal flaw in the second son of the fourth generation was not that he lacked ambition. For Charles Francis Adams Jr., the most Adams by standard definition of the four brothers, frankly admitted that he coveted power. After distinguished service in the Union Army—rising from lieutenant to brigadier general in command of a regiment of Negro cavalry—he sought out the best avenue to position in society, and settled on the railroads. Although he was to rise to titular leadership in his chosen profession, he had not chosen wisely. In the slippery world of Gould, Fisk, and Vanderbilt, he could not overcome being an Adams. He was the first in the family ever to have set out to make money. It was, in his words, "a rather low instinct."[98] And the fact that he was unsuited for it made it a poor vehicle for power.

When Jay Gould cornered the Erie Railroad, Charles Adams described him as "strongly marked by his disposition for silent intrigue. . . . There was a reminiscence of a spider in his nature."[99] Soon Gould would spin his web around the unsuspecting Adams. In 1884, while the Union Pacific was under congressional investigation, Gould suddenly stepped aside as president of the railroad and Adams took over its management. Appointment of the illustrious name with its inherited aura of incorruptibility was all the assurance Congress needed to drop its probe of Gould's illegal manipulations. But six years later, when Gould was ready to regain control of the line, Adams was the helpless fly. It was no contest. Adams's dream of power abruptly ended, and he retired to more scholarly pursuits.

Even while locked in unequal combat with Gould, Adams found time to write a two-volume biography of Richard Henry Dana. In retirement, he devoted most of his leisure to research into early Massachusetts history. He also published a biography of his father, greatly to the displeasure of brothers Henry and Brooks. Charles had never liked Brooks, but in his early years his relationship with Henry had been intimate. However, as their paths diverged the closeness gave way to a tolerance that was maintained by studiously avoiding a collision course. After the Charles Francis Adams biography appeared, Henry wrote Brooks, "I have sinned myself and deeply, and am no more worthy to be called anything, but, thank my diseased and dyspeptic nervous wreck, I did not assassinate my father."[100] And yet, to the more dispassionate reader, Charles Adams, the son who displayed such deep hatred of his father in his own autobiography, was an objective, even sympathetic biographer.

When Henry Adams returned from London, where he had been his father's secretary during the Civil War, articles poured from his pen—attacks on the Grant administration, Congress, political rings, monetary policies, the railroads. He even published a piece debunking the legend of Captain John Smith and Pocahontas. His style reminded the editor of *The Nation* of old John Quincy Adams's "peculiar powers as an assailant . . . an instinct for the jugular and carotid artery as unerring as that of any carnivorous animal."[101]

Life was exciting. He was named one of the three best dancers in Washington. He was appointed assistant professor of history at Harvard and editor of the *North American Review,* a journal of minuscule circulation and mighty influence. He was an idol-breaking editor: "Write thirty pages of abuse of people and houses in England"; "Put more energy into the literary notices"; "Stand on your head and spit at someone"; "Rake up a heap of old family scandals." He was an equally stimulating teacher. When asked how the popes were elected in the eleventh century, he replied, "Pretty much as it pleased God." What is transubstantiation? "Good heavens! How should I know? Look it up." John Adams? "Gentlemen, John Adams was a demagogue."[102] Henry Cabot Lodge, Percy Belmont, and his other students idolized him.

And to add to life's joy, in 1872 he married Marian "Clover" Hooper. To Henry, his Boston bride "is certainly not handsome; nor would she be quite called plain, I think. She is twenty-eight years old. She knows her own mind uncommon well. . . . Her manners are quiet. She reads German—also Latin—also, I fear, a little Greek, but very little. She talks garrulously, but on the whole pretty sensibly. . . . She dresses badly. She decidedly has humor. . . . She has enough money to be quite independent."[103] (When Charles heard that his brother might marry a Hooper, he exclaimed, "Heavens!—No!—they're all crazy as coots. She'll kill herself, just like her aunt!")[104]

The young couple spent their honeymoon on a barge on the Nile and their years commuting between Boston, London, and Washington. They gathered a circle of fascinating friends: the poet-statesman John Hay, the geologist Clarence King, the novelist Henry James, the zoologist Alexander Agassiz. They started to build a town house on Lafayette Square next door to Hay. These were also productive years. Henry's brilliant biography of Albert Gallatin appeared in 1879, along with three volumes of Gallatin's writings, which he edited; a satirical novel of Washington life, *Democracy*, was anonymously published in 1880[105]; his biography of John Randolph appeared in 1882; in 1884 and 1885 he privately printed the first two volumes of his *History of the United States*. Then on December 6, 1885, Marian Adams, an accomplished photographer, after a long period of mental depression during which her mind dwelled on nothing but self-destruction, killed herself by swallowing photographic chemicals.

In response to a letter of sympathy, Henry wrote: "I have found myself strengthened by two thoughts. One was that life could have no other experience so crushing. The other was that at least I had got out of life all the pleasure it had to give. I admit that fate at last has smashed the life out of me; but for twelve years I had everything I most wanted on earth."[106]

Henry Adams lived on. He even indulged in a relationship with the beautiful and fascinating Elizabeth Cameron, unhappy wife of a U.S. senator, which Henry's most thorough biographer feels may well have been ("after the passionate sighings"), for reasons of "Puritan scruple or diminishing ardor, that anomaly in nature, a Platonic one."[107] Yet except for one short period when he became interested in the cause of Cuban independence, he was never again involved in the present. Later, during John Hay's incumbency as secretary of state, Adams had a passive yet valuable function in American statecraft: the two friends took afternoon walks, and Henry's whimsical gloom braced the diplomat against the unalloyed optimism of President Theodore Roosevelt.

But he could never be pulled back into the mainstream of his century. Instead he directed his passion to wandering. With the artist John La Farge he explored the Orient and the islands of the Pacific; he met Robert Louis Stevenson in Samoa and wrote a book on Tahiti; he explored Cuba with Clarence King and the American West with Hay. He spent long periods

Charles Francis Adams, 1807–1886, in a caricature that appeared in *Vanity Fair*, London, 1872, at the time of the *Alabama* Claims Tribunal.

in France. With the Lodges and their poet son Bay he discovered the great Gothic cathedrals. And from these lonely years came his two masterpieces, *Mont-Saint-Michel and Chartres* and *The Education of Henry Adams.*

THE LIFE OF THE youngest of the fourth generation, Brooks Adams, was almost a parody of his imposing ancestors'. He bent to the breaking point their theories of government, and he twisted their eccentricities into near madness. Yet there was still a rampaging genius somewhere in him. As philosophy, his *The Law of Civilization and Decay* was a significant development in seeking formula to explain history, and proved him one of the first to recognize the effect of geography on politics.

Brooks Adams was always strange. As an eleven-year-old, his mother wrote of him: "Papa reads aloud for an hour or two evenings, & poor Brooks screams, & laughs, & rants, & twists, & jumps, & worries about so, that we have been obliged to set him on a footstool, in the middle of the room. He wears the furniture out so badly."[108] In his freshman year at Harvard he was caught cheating on a Latin examination; later brother Charles caught him billing sizable quantities of wine to his account.

There is an apocryphal tale that when a young lady turned down his proposal of marriage, Brooks could not believe that an Adams had been rejected. On her repeating her decision, he promptly left, giving as his final opinion, "Why you perfect damn fool."[109] Brooks finally married Evelyn "Daisy" Davis.[110] It is said that this union came about in an equally unreal fashion. He is supposed to have told Mrs. Henry Cabot Lodge, "If I could find a woman like you, I would marry her instantly." Mrs. Lodge suggested her sister, and Brooks was true to his word. But first he warned Miss Davis that he "was an eccentric almost to the point of madness" and she would have to marry him "on her own responsibility and at her own risk."[111] He was to call his wife *affectionately* "idiot from hell." But the gentle and gracious Daisy was pleased to escape from genteel poverty into such a distinguished family. She did as much as any woman could for Brooks while managing to spend all but her last years outside a mental institution.

With each passing year Brooks Adams became more gruff, irascible, and argumentative. His friend Theodore Roosevelt wrote to John Hay, "He [Brooks] is having a delightful time here, and simply revelling in gloom over the appalling social and civic disasters which he sees impending." It became a ritual for Brooks and Henry to predict the end of the world. Brooks said 1926. Henry said 1917. Brooks said 1911. Henry said 1913. Brooks said, "The world is done"; Henry replied, "The world is done. Of course it is!" Brooks was perfectly serious; Henry only partly so, and then with a wink. Charles Francis, who never liked Brooks anyway, told Henry, "Though I do not share the fears and apprehensions of my brother Brooks, and though I do not think the world is going to come to an end,—I know I am."[112]

Brooks loved Henry. After his sainted father had passed on there was no one but Henry who could understand him. "You have been my good genius." Henry respected his brother's intellect and was powerfully influenced by his theory of history. "I have sought all my life those truths which this mighty infant, this seer unblest, has struck with the agony and bloody sweat of genius." Yet Henry could not stand to be with Brooks. The torrent of words, ideas, concepts left him exhausted. He wrote a friend, "My irritability has become so acute that I have to grind my teeth and bite my tongue whenever Brooks talks with me. He is my double, and you know how I exasperate myself."[113] He invented any excuse to flee from Brooks. Brooks got married; Henry went to Ottawa. Brooks went to Washington; Henry escaped to Paris.

If the world was "done," as Henry and Brooks agreed, they disagreed on what to about it. Brooks was the activist. Henry had given up. Henry preferred to live in the twelfth century. Brooks was anxious to fight on in the twentieth. "I am morally certain," Brooks told Henry, "that men are losing energy—mental energy I mean—very fast—so fast that you can trace the shrinkage from year to year." But Henry wrote him, "I fear you must get some other help than mine for your efforts to protect mankind and ourselves."[114] And so, with the fabled Adams energy, Brooks would go it alone. He would pump the energy back into the man: as a teacher at Boston Law School; as a writer of books and magazine articles; as an unsolicited adviser to his brother-in-law, Senator Lodge, and to President Roosevelt; even as a political candidate. Brooks ran for the Massachusetts legislature but lost by two votes—his uncles Chardon and Shephard Brooks voted against him.

There was a strong streak of mysticism in Brooks Adams. "What I produce I do not manufacture—I find." When he forwarded a manuscript to Henry, he wrote, "What I send you is rough stone. It comes that way out of the ground. I can't control it."[115] What he dredged up was a pastiche of fascistic ideas: racist theories, the inferiority of the Orientals, hatred of the Jews; authoritarian concepts of government; schemes for dividing society by class.

In 1917, as the last public act of the fourth generation, Brooks was elected to the Massachusetts Constitutional Convention. It was 138 years after John Adams had written Massachusetts' first constitution. The delegates were silent in order to hear the words of his great-grandson:

> To carry on anything great . . . we need to establish something close
> to dictatorship. The United States government cannot keep pace with
> the age. Mr. President . . . democracy ought to and must perish.[116]

The same convention that listened in amazement to Brooks's polemics also contained another Adams—his nephew Charles Francis, the son of the unsuccessful Democratic leader. The young Adams had been elected by the largest number of votes cast for a delegate at large. "One hates to believe that an Adams can be popular," commented the *New York Times*.[117]

The fifth-generation Adams looked like his forebears—short of stature, balding, with the large nose and narrow and severe mouth.[118] Yet he was unique in one sense: he was to be the end of America's greatest political dynasty.

After graduating from Harvard, where he was class president and earned the lifelong nickname "Deacon," Charles Francis Adams went to Europe for a year. Instead of using the time abroad to search his soul, as Uncle Henry had done, he went to study English yacht racing! (But this too was in his heritage, for an ancestor of his Crowninshield mother had built the first American yacht.)[119] The Deacon would become one of the country's finest yachtsmen. Most of his boats were named with a double *o*—*Papoose, Baboon, Gossoon, Harpoon*. However, it was in the *Resolute* that he won his greatest race by defeating Sir Thomas Lipton's *Shamrock IV* for the 1920 America's Cup.

Charles Francis became a lawyer, married Frances Lovering, a congress-man's daughter, and, only six years out of Harvard, was named the university's treasurer. He served from 1898 to 1929, increasing the school's endowment fund from $12 million to $100 million. Twice he was also elected mayor of Quincy on the Democratic ticket. But he was no more devoted to party labels than his ancestors had been. When he was selected, without his knowledge, by the 1920 Democratic State Convention as a candidate for presidential elector, he asked to have his name withdrawn from the official ballot—he was going to vote for Harding! Later he advocated that presidents be limited to a single six-year term and be required to renounce party affiliation.

On his appointment as secretary of the navy in 1929 he was so politically unknown that many mistook him for Charles Francis "Pop" Adams, an improbably remote cousin who was an owner of the Boston Braves and Boston Bruins.[120] The nautical post was a natural for the "right" Adams: not only had great-great-grandfather John Adams founded the American navy but great-grandfather Benjamin W. Crowninshield had been Madison's secretary of the navy, and his brother Jacob Crowninshield had been confirmed as Jefferson's secretary of the navy (although he never served). So Charles Francis Adams resigned from over forty corporate directorships and went to Washington, where each day he waited his turn in the cafeteria for navy beans. (In reality, he said, they were Boston beans.) Once a week, reported the *New York Times* on its front page, "Secretary Adams has a [cod] fish ball with his beans."[121]

If the menu pleased him, the persistence of reporters and photographers did not. Once, when ordered by the photographers to sit at his desk and "write something," they discovered that what he was writing was "This is hell this is hell this is hell."[122] Yet reporters sometimes found that his wry humor made good copy. At the London Naval Conference of 1930 the "Topics of the Times" told how "he was seen, the other day, sailing a number of toy boats in the waters of Kensington Garden, in the heart of London! The implication is obvious. The Secretary of the American Navy, having had all his large ships torpedoed by insidious foreign diplomats, is forced to concentrate on toy models in an artificial lake."[123]

His regime at the Navy Department was a conservative one. He wished to bring the fleet up to the parity allowed by the 1930 conference, but President Hoover ordered retrenchment as the Great Depression began, and the navy's strength fell far behind the quotas permitted by international agreement. At one time it was reported that Adams's relations with the president were almost at the breaking point. Hoover, however, professed profound admiration for his secretary of the navy, and in his memoirs wrote, "Had I known him better earlier, I should have made him Secretary of State."[124]

When Franklin Delano Roosevelt entered the White House, Adams returned to corporate management and sailing. In 1939, at the age of seventy-three, he won the King's, Astor, and Puritan Cups, the three most coveted domestic racing trophies, in a single season. It was as if a twelve-year-old horse had captured the Triple Crown. He died in 1954 at the right age for an Adams, eighty-seven.

The Deacon's son, the fourth Charles Francis Adams, married Margaret Stockton, daughter of the president of the First National Bank of Boston, a direct descendant of the New Jersey political dynasty, and became chairman of the board of the Raytheon Company, a major defense and space equipment supplier. "To the best of my knowledge," he wrote in response to a query, "no members of the family are active in political life."[125]

The Adamses had several explanations for their political demise. John Adams might even have contended that it was a *planned* exodus to higher forms of cultural expression. While serving as "militia diplomat" in France, he wrote Abigail, "I must study politics and war that my sons may have liberty to study mathematics and philosophy. My sons ought to study mathematics and philosophy . . . in order to give their children a right to study painting, poetry, music, architecture."[126] This theory of politics to poetry in three generations turned out to be a fairly accurate prediction. Yet how would the second president have explained that in the fourth generation, his heirs had "retrogressed" to commerce?

It was the opinion of Brooks Adams that "a single family can stay adjusted through three generations." He then added, "It is now full four generations since John Adams wrote the Constitution of Massachusetts. It is time that we perished. The world is tired of us."[127]

Other causes contributed to the family's fall as a political dynasty. Wealth—usually a distinct aid in dynasty building—played a strange trick on the Adamses, and seemed to remove some of the spur to political involvement. The ever-present eccentricities, accentuated in each successive generation, made them less appealing to the electorate. And they had just plain bad luck from a dynastic standpoint—Henry and Brooks were childless—although there were still enough Adamses to have carried on if they had wished to. But most important, the dynasty simply lost its zest for public service. Even as early as the third generation, Charles Francis Adams referred to his distinguished career as minister to Great Britain as "my eight years of purgatory in public office."[128] By the fifth generation, Secretary of the Navy Charles Francis Adams would consider politics more an act of civic-mindedness, like giving to the Community Chest, and as a tithe to one's ancestors, than as an end in itself.

Yet for a century and a half the direct descendants of a simple Quincy farmer were prominently involved in the political fabric of their country. Through election and appointment they played a leading role in every major development in American history, from the fight for independence through the fight to abolish slavery. When Sir Francis Galton wrote his classic study of hereditary genius, he rated the Adamses as the only American family worthy of inclusion.[129]

SEVENTEEN

The
Kennedy
DYNASTY

Joe [Junior] was supposed to be the politician. When he died, I took
his place. If anything happened to me, Bobby would take my place.
If something happened to Bobby, Teddy would take his place.
—JOHN F. KENNEDY[1]

A REMARKABLE FAMILY: the first Irish Catholics of great wealth
in America, making most of their fortune in real estate; prominent in politics, having three members of the same generation in
Congress and two members in Congress at the same time; outstanding in
the affairs of their church, while socially advantaged enough to marry into
English aristocracy.

Each of these achievements was shared later by the Kennedys, but this
description first fitted the Carrolls of Maryland. These early Irish Catholic
Brahmins were descended from an ancient family of Irish princes. Arriving
in America a half century after the landing of the Pilgrims, the Carrolls
came to Maryland under the patronage of Lord Baltimore during the reign
of King James II.[2]

By the time of the American Revolution they owned most of the land
on which the city of Washington was later built.[3] John Adams was particu-
larly impressed by their wealth; having just arrived in Philadelphia for the
opening of the first Continental Congress, he wrote in his diary: "This day

Mr. Chase introduced to us a Mr. Carroll, of Annapolis, a very sensible gentleman, a Roman Catholic, and of the first fortune in America. His income is ten thousand pounds sterling a year now, will be fourteen in two or three years, they say; besides, his father has a vast estate which will be his after his father."[4] Daniel Carroll signed the Articles of Confederation and his cousin Charles of Carrollton, Adams's friend, signed the Declaration of Independence. As he did so another delegate observed, "There go a few millions."[5]

Yet the influence of this first great Irish Catholic dynasty ended decades before the progenitor of the second great Irish Catholic dynasty—with its superficially similar record of achievement—arrived in the United States.

After the generation of the founding fathers, only two Carrolls were elected to high office. The family preferred caste privilege to leadership. The granddaughters of Charles Carroll of Carrollton, anticipating the later flurry of matches between rich American ladies and titled Englishmen, became the Duchess of Leeds, the Marchioness of Wellesley, and the Baroness Stafford. For their beauty and charm the three were known in London as the "American Graces."

The Carrolls were part of a trickle of Irishmen who had been emigrating to America throughout the seventeenth and eighteenth centuries. Then in the late 1840s, with the sudden failure of the potato crop, it became a cascade, washing up to 216,000 immigrants a year into the ports of New York and Boston at the high-water mark. These new arrivals were unwelcome and, except for their brawn, unwanted. As the factory gates posted "No Irish Need Apply," the Irish applied themselves to politics, the one area in which their numbers were meaningful and their gregarious talents of value.

Prejudice channeled families like the Fitzgeralds and the Kennedys into public life by closing to them the more significant private life of the country, but this led in time to the election of the first Catholic president of the United States, an event that sociologist E. Digby Baltzell called "a turning point in our history and symbol of a trend toward ethnic aristocracy in America."[6]

IT WAS NOT THE blight of the potato, the legendary Great Hunger, that brought to America the great-grandfather of President Kennedy and his senator brothers. He came from Dunganstown, County Wexford, in the southeast corner of Ireland, which was relatively prosperous and unaffected by the horror that was then sweeping other parts of the country. What probably caused Patrick Kennedy in October 1848 to travel the six miles from his home to the port of New Ross and board a ship for America was the fact that he was a youngest son. After the family had satisfied the demands of the landlord there would be little left over to start him on a farm of his own, even if land had been available. So he arrived in Boston, became a maker of whiskey barrels, and died of cholera fourteen years later—no richer than if he had remained in Ireland.[7]

Another young man from County Wexford arrived in Boston at about the same time. Thomas Fitzgerald became a farm laborer for $6 a month and then the proprietor of a grocery and liquor store in the North End, not far from Paul Revere's house. He too died in his early thirties.

In the next generation the Fitzgeralds and the Kennedys would be alternately political enemies and allies in the constantly shifting mosaic of Boston politics; in the following generation they would permanently unite in marriage (though not always in politics); and in the fourth generation the Kennedy-Fitzgerald genes would have national impact.

JOHN FRANCIS FITZGERALD AND Patrick Joseph Kennedy, the grandfathers who gave their names to a president, were as different as the nicknames by which they were known. Fitzgerald was "Honey Fitz"—an appellation that would have befitted a vaudeville song-and-dance man; Kennedy was known as "P.J.," in the manner that imposing executives are referred to by underlings who would not think of addressing them familiarly by their first names.

Grandfather Kennedy, recalled the future president, "wouldn't let us cut up or even wink in his presence."[8] This austere and awesome figure was about five feet ten inches tall, weighed 185 pounds, and had sandy hair, blue eyes, and a luxuriously curled mustache. First a stevedore and longshoreman, he soon took over a saloon in Haymarket Square. But this barkeep rarely lifted a glass. Without cursing or raising his voice, he maintained order; brawlers would not be tolerated. Eventually P.J. acquired an interest in three saloons, a wholesale liquor company, a coal company, and a local bank. Joseph Kennedy, his only son, was not raised in need; his father owned a sixty-foot cabin cruiser, the *Eleanor.*

In Boston of the 1880s it was as predictable for an Irish saloonkeeper to go into politics as it had been for an earlier generation of Yankees to go sea or to the counting house. P. J. Kennedy became a three-time member of Democratic presidential conventions and was six times elected to office, five as a member of the Massachusetts House of Representatives and once as a state senator. But his overriding interest was in East Boston, which he ran as a neighborly welfare state. Being its boss, he was automatically a member of the four-man "Board of Strategy," the "mayor-makers" who picked Democratic candidates for citywide office and ran Boston. Another member of the "board" was John Francis Fitzgerald. Kennedy privately considered him insufferable.

For a man with P. J. Kennedy's sense of dignity, working with Honey Fitz must have been unbearable. Here was a bantam rooster of a man— short, cocky, strutting, yet handsome, though his mouth was narrow and his eyes a little too close together; a study in perpetual motion, organizing dances, dancing with the wallflowers; an Irish chipmunk with just a trace of brogue, chattering away at 200 words a minute; always turning up uninvited, always singing (except at wakes), generally off key; always weeping— when it suited him; every inch the charming rogue. Politicians despised him. Ladies adored him.

It suited Honey Fitz's purpose to recount a youth of hardship. The facts were otherwise. He graduated from the famed Boston Latin School, a contemporary of Santayana and Berenson, captained a polo team, and even attended Harvard Medical School until the death of his father forced him to drop out in the first year. Next he took a civil service examination, came out near the top of the list, and went to work as a custom house clerk. Honey Fitz later founded a prosperous insurance business, and in 1892 he was elected to the state Senate. Reporters branded him "the North End Napoleon." The name so pleased him that he assumed mannerisms of the French emperor. He was now undisputed boss of the North End and one-fourth of the Board of Strategy.

In 1894 Fitzgerald, although opposed by Kennedy, was elected to Congress. He was the only Democratic congressman from New England and the only Catholic in the House of Representatives. During his six consecutive years in Washington he earned a reputation as an insistent and irrelevant debater and an effective bread-and-butter fighter for Boston Harbor. He won his third term despite his opponent's charge that he was a carpetbagger, since he had moved to respectable Concord, twenty-five miles from his North End constituents.

Congressman Fitzgerald also became a publisher. He bought the *Republic* for $500 and turned it into an Irish American social weekly. Readers didn't flock to it, but advertisers who needed political favors did. The congressman-publisher was soon netting $25,000 a year. (In 1914, when Walter Lippmann, Herbert Croly, and Walter Weyl decided to found a journal of liberal opinion, they discovered that an obscure Boston weekly already had their chosen title and were forced to name their magazine the *New Republic*.[9])

But Congress was only a curtain-raiser for the job that really counted—mayor of Boston. In 1905 Honey Fitz became His Honor, the Mayor—again against the wishes of P. J. Kennedy. Fitzgerald was not the first Irishman to hold the post; two outstanding mayors, Hugh O'Brien and Patrick Collins, had preceded him. He was, however, the city's first Irish American mayor to be born in this country, and, as James Michael Curley pointed out, he was the first Boston mayor without beard or mustache.

In the year that Fitzgerald was elected mayor there were more persons of Irish extraction in Boston than in Dublin, an estimated 60 percent of the city's population. The mayor's hold over his fellow Boston Irish was re-counted by Curley, who was ten years younger than Honey Fitz and carved of harder rock. Teaching a class on naturalization for Irish immigrants, Curley asked a student to tell him who made the laws of the nation.

"John F. Fitzgerald." Who then, Curley wanted to know, made the laws of the state? "John F. Fitzgerald," the young man answered again. And who is the president of the United States? "John F. Fitzgerald."

"If I hadn't stopped the man there, I'm sure he would have gone on to tell me that John F. drove the snakes out of Ireland and discovered America."[10]

During his first two years in office, Mayor Fitzgerald attended 1,200 dinners, 1,500 dances, 200 picnics, and 1,000 meetings. He made 3,000 speeches and danced with 5,000 girls. If Honey Fitz were to be wakened in the dead of night and asked to speak on any subject under the sun, wrote a *Boston Post* reporter, "he will readily, not to say willingly, arise from his couch, slip his frock coat over his pajamas and speak eloquently for two hours and seventeen minutes on that subject."[11]

The Honey Fitz administration may have been an artistic success, but it did not please the city's good-government element. "Our present Mayor," said a Baptist minister from Roxbury, "has the distinction of appointing more saloonkeepers and bartenders to public office than any previous mayor."[12] A physician was removed from the Board of Health to make room for a saloonkeeper; liquor dealers were appointed as superintendent of public buildings and wire commissioner; a whitewasher became superintendent of sewers; a bartender who had been expelled from the legislature was named superintendent of streets. Civil service regulations were circumvented by the invention of such job categories as tea warmer, tree climber, rubber-boot repairers, and watchmen to watch the watchmen. Brother Henry Fitzgerald was put in charge of patronage; brother Jim Fitzgerald was given a valuable liquor license; brother Michael Fitzgerald, a Charlestown policeman, was paid $1,100 a year to carry a daily traffic report from the Warren Avenue Bridge to City Hall, earning a reputation as "the human postage stamp."

The city discovered that under its charming mayor it had been defrauded of $200,000 by a single coal company; that it was paying sixty cents a barrel above the going price for cement; that bids and contracts for city work were often accepted verbally; that bills and vouchers had mysteriously disappeared; that there were dozens of strange land deals.

Meanwhile, back at the *Republic,* things were flourishing. Advertising rates in ratio to circulation were perhaps the highest in the country, while its advertisers, wrote Francis Russell, "read like a summary of the Boston Stock Exchange."[13] In one issue of Honey Fitz's newspaper Boston banks bought fourteen pages of advertising.

Mayor Fitzgerald was defeated in 1907.

The "better elements," made bold by their victory, doubled the mayoralty term to four years. So in 1909 Honey Fitz bounced back to beat a Beacon Street Yankee by 1,402 votes.

The second term recorded some solid achievements—a City Hall annex, an aquarium, a zoo, a high school of commerce—while "banned in Boston" became a legend. Honey Fitz outlawed the turkey trot and the tango as immoral, and *Salome* as sacrilegious. He also introduced a theme song, "Sweet Adeline," a popular hit of the day, which his daughter Rose had taught him. He became known as the only man who could sing the ballad when cold sober and get away with it. Franklin D. Roosevelt once greeted him as "Dulce Adelina," claiming that after a Honey Fitz tour of South America the natives thought it was the national anthem.

For a man known to have made thirty speeches in one night, there was little time left over for family life. When Honey Fitz spent an evening with his wife and children because a magazine wanted to do a story on the mayor at home, Mrs. Fitzgerald told him, "John, it does indeed seem refreshing to have you here. I am not sorry you are to have photographs taken to mark the evening. I am going to frame one and place a card over it on which I will write: 'Taken on his evening at home.'" Mary Fitzgerald, a slender and erect woman, with fair hair and luminous brown eyes, a horror of ostentation, and a fear of publicity, was in charge of bringing up the three boys and three girls. "I want my home to be a place of inspiration and encouragement to all my family," she told the magazine writer. "I am a home woman in every way."[14]

Since Mrs. Fitzgerald shrank from the public glare that her husband basked in, Honey Fitz drafted his pretty daughter Rose to act as his official hostess. Between his terms at City Hall she had been studying in a European convent. She was now a poised young woman with a deeply religious outlook and a command of music and foreign languages. She accompanied her father to political rallies, banquets, and wakes. At sixteen she presided over her first ship launching. She greeted President William Howard Taft and other celebrities. There was even a rumor that she was engaged to Sir Thomas Lipton.

At a dinner that Mayor Fitzgerald gave in 1912 for the City Council, James Michael Curley, uninvited, slipped into the room and used Honey Fitz's forum to announce his own candidacy for mayor. Under withering attack from the young challenger, Fitzgerald withdrew from the race. He had no stomach for this sort of contest. Curley had developed a toughness from his slum youth that was totally lacking in Fitzgerald. Fitzgerald wanted to have fun and Curley wanted to have power. Curley's rise signified the end of petty political barons like John F. Fitzgerald and P. J. Kennedy. He wanted to, and would, control the city; they only wanted their shares, and had neither the cunning nor the ability to stem the class bitterness that he adroitly manipulated.

After Fitzgerald left City Hall he often ran for political office. But his luck and timing had run out. Notre Dame awarded Honey Fitz an honorary degree in 1915, and, as "Dr. Fitzgerald," as he now liked to be called, he ran for the U.S. Senate against Henry Cabot Lodge Sr. in 1916. He went down to Washington and sat in his august opponent's seat in the Senate chamber. "It feels natural," he declared.[15] But the *New York Times* declared that Fitzgerald was turning the election into a joke, calling him "this amiable kisser of the Blarney Stone, warbler of 'Sweet Adeline,' rider of Florida sharks, a butterfly flitting unconcerned around the solid men of Boston."[16] The electorate agreed, but by a slim margin of 33,000 votes.

He hoped to make a comeback by opposing Curley for mayor in 1917. The notion was short-lived, however, after the irrepressible James Michael announced he planned a series of addresses, including one titled "Great Lovers: From Cleopatra to Toodles." Toodles, whose last name was Ryan, was a shapely blond cigarette girl at the Ferncroft Inn on the Newburyport Turnpike. Rumor mentioned her alongside Honey Fitz and even linked them in an anonymous limerick. The former mayor, who righteously insisted that there was no fire to match the smoke, quickly backed out of the race. Curley's "Great Lovers" remained just the title of an undelivered speech.[17]

Family tree is TO COME

Family tree is TO COME

Family tree is TO COME

Family tree is TO COME

Honey Fitz did make a comeback of sorts in 1918 when he was elected to the House of Representatives by 238 votes. His opponent's manager, Joe Kane, who was also Joseph P. Kennedy's first cousin (their mothers were sisters), carried the fight to Washington. He charged that Fitzgerald's election was "by means of the fraudulent votes of the liquor dealers, bartenders, and city job holders illegally registered in his ward, and in the padded returns of alleged residents in the cheap lodging houses."[18] A congressional committee agreed and Honey Fitz was removed from office. Unperturbed, he announced, "There are half a dozen men in the Senate now who were unseated in recent years, while Mr. McKinley, who was unseated in the 48th Congress, was afterwards elected President."[19]

Four years later Honey Fitz was defeated for governor in a race that was of little significance except that it provided John Fitzgerald Kennedy with his earliest political memories: he toured the wards with his grandfather. At seventy-nine, in 1942, the old warhorse was entered against Representative Joseph Casey in the Democratic primary for U.S. senator to face Republican Henry Cabot Lodge Jr. Honey Fitz might have won the primary, thought Joe Kane, but Joseph P. Kennedy, his father-in-law, decided against putting up the $200,000 to $300,000 that would have been necessary to wage a successful campaign.

Honey Fitz lived long enough to sing "Sweet Adeline" at the celebration of his grandson's first election to Congress in 1946. He died in 1950, two years before Jack Kennedy righted an old family score by defeating Senator Henry Cabot Lodge Jr. His wife, however, was able to celebrate the inauguration of her grandson as the first Catholic president. She was never told of his death in Dallas. "I had a hunch she knew," said her son Thomas, "but we never talked about it."[20] She died on August 8, 1964, at the age of ninety-eight.

HONEY FITZ WAS NOT pleased when Rose married Joseph P. Kennedy in 1914. He felt that the daughter of a famous mayor should do better than the son of a ward boss and saloon owner. His own candidate for son-in-law was a wealthy contractor.

The young man who had married into the Fitzgerald family was a graduate of Boston Latin and Harvard, class of 1912. Robert Benchley later described their class as having produced "only one Bishop of Albania," "only one member who caught a giant panda" (Kermit Roosevelt), and only one "village clerk of Hewlett Harbor, L.I."[21] Joe Kennedy didn't make the best clubs, nor did Harvard ever give him an honorary degree or a place on its board of overseers. But by the time he was twenty-five he was being described in the press as the youngest bank president in the nation—though of a tiny Boston bank in which his father held substantial stock. It was Joe's ambition to be a millionaire by thirty-five, an ambition he easily realized. At the twentieth reunion of his Harvard class Kennedy listed his occupation as capitalist. In a lifetime of moneymaking the capital came primarily from four sources: the movies, the stock market, liquor, and real estate.

—*The movies.* In the mid-1920s Kennedy invested in a chain of New England theaters, which eventually led him to the production side of the business. He moved himself (but not his family) to Hollywood in 1928 where three companies were each paying $2,000 a week for his executive ability. He produced a series of films starring Gloria Swanson and arranged the merger that created RKO.[22] "After thirty-two months in the movies," wrote biographer Richard J. Whalen, "he was more than thirty pounds underweight—and perhaps five million dollars richer."[23]

—*The stock market.* In the roaring bull market of the late 1920s Joe Kennedy was a loner and a speculator. "He became a wizard of such tricky stock dodges as market rigging, matched orders, margin manipulation, and washed and short sales."[24] Then in the summer of 1929 he suddenly left the market. Years later, reporter Joseph Dinneen asked him why. "Very simply," answered Kennedy, "I dropped in at a shoeshine parlor on Wall Street. The boy who shined my shoes did not know me. . . . He looked up at me as he snapped the cloth over my shoes and told me what was going to happen to various stocks and offerings on the market that day. I listened as I looked down at him, and when I left the place I thought: 'When a time comes that a shoeshine boy knows as much as I do about what is going on in the stock market, tells me so and is entirely correct, there is something the matter either with me or with the market and it's time for me to get out,' and I did."[25] When the crash came in October 1929 the Kennedy fortune was unaffected. He had kept his huge movie profits in cash.

—*Liquor.* It was apparent in 1933 that the amendment repealing Prohibition would soon become law, and the competition became intense for the rights to represent the British distillers in America. That September Mr. and Mrs. Joseph Kennedy went to Europe with Mr. and Mrs. James Roosevelt. The president's son and his friends were royally received by the English liquor interests. When they returned home, Joe Kennedy was the U.S. agent for Haig and Haig, John Dewar, and Gordon's Gin. Three months before Prohibition ended his warehouses were overflowing with liquor that had been shipped into the country under "medicinal" licenses issued in Washington. "The British didn't select their agents haphazardly," said a rival distributor. "They felt Jimmy Roosevelt was a good connection, so they gave their lines to Kennedy." If Jimmy expected to go into the business as a partner, he was mistaken. When Kennedy's firm, Somerset Importers, was incorporated, Joe had no partners. He replied to critics, "Kennedy was doing all right by himself before he ever met Jimmy Roosevelt."[26] The original Kennedy investment in the liquor business was $100,000. He sold the company in 1946 for $8 million in cash.

—*Real estate.* Ironically, when Joe Kennedy tried to play it safe he made more money than ever before. Expecting hard times, he started to put his money into real estate, primarily on Manhattan island. His agent estimated he made $100 million. It was Joe's practice to move into a promising situation, exploit it, and then quickly move out. He bought one property at Fifty-Ninth Street and Lexington Avenue for $1,900,000—only $100,000 in cash—and sold it for $6 million. The one building that Kennedy held on to was Chicago's Merchandise Mart, which he bought in 1945 for $12,956,516, approximately $1,000,000 down; by 1966 it was valued at $75,000,000, with annual rentals in excess of Kennedy's original purchase price.

Fortune magazine's survey of multimillionaires in 1957 estimated Kennedy's fortune above $250,000,000, in a class with Irenée and William Du Pont, Howard Hughes, and Sid Richardson. He was one of the few of the astronomically wealthy whose money didn't stem from inheritance or oil. And Kennedy's fortune was different in another way. As one of his intimates said, "It isn't paper. It's real. Joe could write a check for nine million dollars just like that."[27]

Yet here was a capitalist who stood apart from the system. His wealth wasn't derived from finance, production, or distribution. His money wasn't used to create goods. No product bore the name Kennedy. This standing apart from the business community—and generally holding it in low regard—was to play a significant role in shaping his children. Unlike many self-made men, who take pride in what they create and wish their sons to perpetuate it, Kennedy led his sons away from his business and into public service.

MANY COULD NOT SEE the man for the money. Those who tried often came away baffled and confused. Joseph P. Kennedy was complex, by nature a pessimist, yet he held the most extraordinarily optimistic dream for his family; he was well educated, with a refined taste in music, yet he was addicted to the crudest racial epithets; he could display the quickest, most infectious grin and the most explosive temper; he was a dictatorial executive and a maudlin emotionalist, openhanded and closefisted.

At home during the children's youth he was the very model of a model Victorian pater familias: his word was law. But he wasn't home very often. It was not until a month after the birth of Patricia that Joe saw his new daughter. He was otherwise occupied at the Waldorf, stabilizing the stock of the Yellow Cab Company.

In 1915 Joe Jr. was born. John was born two years later. Then came, during the twenties, in rapid succession, Rosemary, Kathleen, Eunice, Patricia, Robert, and Jean. The family named their sailboat *Tenofus*. But with the addition of Edward in 1932 they needed a bigger boat, christened *One More*.

During Joe's absences, there was Rose. Years later, when her sons held three of the highest offices in the land, Adlai Stevenson introduced her at a Washington banquet as "the woman who started it all, the head of the greatest employment agency in America."[28] "She was the glue," said her president son. And then he repeated himself for emphasis.[29] A petite brunette with high cheekbones and a youthful figure ("Now I believe in the stork!" said FDR's son-in-law, John Boettiger, when he saw her at the White House), Rose Kennedy was the vivid presence in her children's first years. She taught them the catechism, heard their prayers, kept a card index on their illnesses, and saw them off to school—at least the eldest ones. She was tough-fibered and slightly aloof. "She was a little removed," recalled Jack, "which I think is the only way to survive when you have nine children."[30] When Joe was around he drove home his philosophy of competition: it's not how you play the game that counts, it's winning. Rose tempered her husband's overdrive, within limits. Years later, writing in her diary, she remembered, "When the children needed to be spanked, I often used a ruler, and sometimes a coat hanger, which was often more convenient because in any room there would be a closet and the hangers in them would be right at hand."[31]

Among the children, Joe was the leader, a natural athlete. "My brother Joe took the greatest interest in us," said Bobby. "He taught us to sail, to swim, to play football and baseball." Added Jack: "Joe made the task of bringing up a large family immeasurably easier for my father and mother, for what they taught him he passed on to us and their teachings were not diluted through him but strengthened."[32] Joe had his mother's good looks and consideration for others, much of his father's drive and capacity for instant anger, his grandfather Honey Fitz's gift of banter. "Joe had so much personality," his college roommate said, "that you could tell he'd entered a room if your back was to the door and he hadn't said a word."[33] Later he enjoyed smoking cigars, going to the racetrack, and talking about becoming the first Catholic president of the United States.

In the shadow of Joe, two years younger, was Jack. The two eldest boys fought constantly. They were altogether different, thought their father. Joe was "more dynamic, more sociable and easy going"; Jack "was rather shy, withdrawn and quiet."[34] His parents were sure he would be a teacher or writer. Bobby, eight years behind Jack, was the smallest, with the poorest physical coordination and the least interest in intellectual pursuits. He was always scrambling to catch up, to be included. As Ethel Kennedy later explained, "The major difference between Bobby and his brothers is that Bobby always had to fight for everything."[35] Teddy was seventeen years younger than his eldest brother, far too little to be considered an equal. He couldn't compete, but he rigged the sailboats for the others and worked hard at being liked.

The eldest of the girls was Rosemary. It was soon apparent that she was not like the other children. Her mother recalled: "She couldn't stay on a sled like the others. She couldn't balance herself on a bicycle. She was slow in school. I went to our family doctor, and then to specialists but there didn't seem to be any answer. . . . In summer, the other youngsters would go out in the boat alone. She couldn't. And she couldn't understand why. It was the same at dancing school. She would come home and say, 'Mother, the boys danced with Eunice and Mary and Jean, but not with me.'"[36] The family tried to include Rosemary in their activities to the extent of her ability. She was even formally presented to the queen when Joe was ambassador to Great Britain. But in her twenty-third year she became irritable and difficult to manage. Doctors told Joe that a lobotomy could relieve his daughter's mood swings. The lobotomy was not successful and left her permanently incapacitated. She remained institutionalized for the rest of her life. The family invented various stories to explain her absence. Rosemary died in 2005, age eighty-six, with her sisters and Ted by her side.

In the world of the Kennedy children the leadership of the girls was assumed by the next oldest, Kathleen. A Frenchman who knew them when they lived in London said, "Eunice is the most intellectual and Pat's the prettiest, but Kathleen is the one you remember."[37]

The Kennedy household was self-contained, a unit set in perpetual motion, once described as an Oklahoma land grab, with everyone racing for his share. "I couldn't keep them straight," remembered Gore Vidal. "They were always running around like so many wire-haired terriers."[38] They sustained each other. The world, as they saw it, consisted of Kennedys and others.

THE FAMILY LEFT BOSTON in the spring of 1926. They would still spend the summers at their rambling, eighteen-room house at Hyannis Port on Cape Cod, but Boston, said the father, was "no place to bring up Catholic children."[39] For the next decade they made their home in the Riverdale and Bronxville suburbs of New York City.

During this period Joe set up trust funds for the children. With subsequent additions, the trusts would earmark upward of $10 million for each child. "I fixed it," Joe said, "so that any of my children, financially speaking, could look me in the eye and tell me to go to hell." The future president considered his father's explanation to be "a myth." "That was in 1929, and he was speculating," said Jack. "It was very risky business. He was speculating pretty hard and his health was not too good at the time, and that was the reason he did it. There was no other reason for it."[40]

Yet despite Joe Kennedy's concentration on moneymaking and the opulence with which he surrounded himself, he talked of wealth not as an end in itself but as a means to uplift his family, a foundation on which to build the next generation. "The measure of a man's success in life is not the money he has made," he said. "It's the kind of family he has raised." Or again: "My wife and I have given nine hostages to fortune. Our children . . . are more important than anything else in the world." This was a constant, recurring theme through all his life and all his public statements. As his friend Arthur Krock of the *New York Times* said, Joseph Kennedy "had a dynastic impulse."[41]

JOE KENNEDY AND FRANKLIN D. Roosevelt first met during World War I when Kennedy was assistant manager of Bethlehem Steel's Fore River Shipyard in Quincy, Massachusetts, and FDR was assistant secretary of the navy. Unlike so many others, Kennedy never underestimated the young Roosevelt—"the hardest trader I'd ever run up against," said Joe.[42] The two men were opposites in background, outlook, and style. Yet in 1932, when Honey Fitz and the Boston Irish politicians supported Al Smith for president—and considered it treason to do otherwise—Kennedy became one of Roosevelt's staunchest backers.

Inherently pessimistic, Kennedy feared the collapse of the economic system, and with it his fortune; and with the collapse of his fortune the economic roof he had built over his family would collapse; and with its collapse would come the end of his dream for his sons. The man who could prevent this, Kennedy reasoned, was Roosevelt, "a man of action . . . [with] the capacity to get things done."[43] He gave $25,000 to the Roosevelt campaign, lent it another $50,000, and raised an additional $100,000. He helped get the nomination for Roosevelt in Chicago by using his influence with his friend William Randolph Hearst, who controlled the key California and Texas delegations, and he later traveled with Roosevelt on his campaign train.

Kennedy confidently expected to be named secretary of the Treasury. Roosevelt had other ideas. Kennedy waited. Finally, after more than a year, the president appointed him to the new Securities and Exchange Commission, with the understanding that he would be its first chairman. The announcement was met with incredulity: the great stock market speculator was to be put in charge of the agency that was to police the stock market. This was like "putting Peter Rabbit to work guarding the cabbage patch," said one Democrat.[44] But Kennedy did a brilliant job at the SEC. Roosevelt next called on him to head the new Maritime Commission. Congress was so eager for him to accept that it passed an unprecedented resolution waiving the requirement that he sell his stock in Todd Shipyard, which would otherwise have been a conflict of interests.

Returning to Harvard that spring for his twenty-fifth reunion, Joe's classmates put on a skit, "In the Good Old Maritime," in which Commissioner Kennedy tells his secretary, "Get me Frank at the White House." He picks up the phone. "I'm here, Frank. It's nine o'clock. Start the country."[45]

Then Joe Kennedy, the grandson of an Irish immigrant, was appointed U.S. ambassador to the Court of St. James's.

Old Honey Fitz, his barrel chest now swelling with pride, was introduced at a dinner of the Boston Chamber of Commerce by Charles Francis Adams. "I told Charley recently," announced Fitzgerald, "that I might go abroad pretty soon to meet the King and Queen, and Wallie and the rest of them, and asked him for some tips. You see, Charley Adams' great-grandfather and his grandfather were ambassadors to Great Britain in times of great stress, too."[46]

———

"THE AMBASSADOR," AS HE was from now on to be called, was at the height of his public career. The English were delighted and amused by the improper Bostonian, his lovely wife, and their nine children. "His bouncing offspring make the most politically ingratiating family since Theodore Roosevelt's," commented *Life* magazine. "Whether or not Franklin Roosevelt thought of it beforehand, it has turned out that when he appointed Mr. Kennedy to be Ambassador to Great Britain he got eleven Ambassadors for the price of one."[47]

As celebrities, the Kennedys were even being satirized in a Broadway musical. Jack, a student at Harvard, saw Victor Moore and Sophie Tucker in *Leave It to Me*, and reported to his parents that "the jokes about us got by far the biggest laughs whatever that signifies."[48]

Washington gossip was that Ambassador Kennedy had White House ambitions. The reasoning went that since FDR was barred by precedent from seeking a third term in 1940, Joe would emerge as a contender doubly blessed by Roosevelt and business. Ernest K. Lindley wrote a magazine article, "Will Kennedy Run for President?"

Yet as Hitler cast his net over Europe, Kennedy threw his prestige behind the "peace at any price" policy of Neville Chamberlain. Never one to keep his opinions a secret, Joe announced: "It has long been a theory of mine that it is unproductive for both the democratic and dictator countries to widen the division now existing between them by emphasizing their difference . . . they could advantageously bend their energies toward solving their common problems by an attempt to re-establish good relations on a world basis."[49]

Kennedy's isolationism was based on a supposition and a desire, according to Harold Ickes, who was witness to an argument Joe and Ambassador to France William Bullitt. Joe's supposition was that Germany was going to win the war; his desire was to save his children.[50]

Why did Roosevelt continue to retain an outspoken "appeaser" as his ambassador? The answer, supplied by columnists Joseph Alsop and Robert Kintner, was that "the President regards Kennedy as likely to do less harm in London than in New York."[51]

When Britain entered the war, Kennedy's days in London were numbered. Roosevelt began bypassing his ambassador and dealing directly with Churchill, the new prime minister. Joe finally resigned after a *Boston Globe* interview, which he thought was off the record, revealed the extent of his isolationism as well as comments on Churchill's fondness for brandy, the king's speech impediment, the queen's housewifely appearance, and Eleanor Roosevelt's notes asking him "to have some little Susie Glotz to tea at the

Embassy."[52] Joseph P. Kennedy was never again to be a political force in his own right.

Nineteen forty was a year of political awakening for his two oldest sons. Two decades later Rose Kennedy would say that her sons were "rocked to political lullabies."[53] But the famous family dinner-table conversations (in later days pictured as almost a junior Algonquin roundtable) were about the men and moves of politics, not substantive issues. Young Jack could write his parents that "tonight is a big night in Boston as the Honorable John F. Fitzgerald is making a speech for his good friend, James Michael," and yet, at the same time, be so little aware of the Great Depression that he asked to be sent the *Literary Digest* "because I did not know about the Market Slump until a long time after.."[54]

Jack Kennedy entered Harvard in 1936, the year Henry Cabot Lodge Jr. was elected to the Senate, and as a student, in the opinion of one of his professors, rated "reasonably inconspicuous."[55] He spent his junior year in Europe, partly working for his father at the embassy, and returned to Harvard imbued with his father's view of the European situation. His senior thesis was titled "Appeasement at Munich: The Inevitable Result of the Slowness of the British Democracy to Change from a Disarmament Policy." Arthur Krock helped get it published and suggested a new title, *Why England Slept*. It was an immediate success, selling 80,000 copies in the United States and England. As publisher Henry Luce wrote in the foreword, it was "a remarkable book" for two reasons: first, because of its "dispassionate" tone; and second, because it was written "by one so young."[56] For the first time the young man had become engaged in public issues, and, while the substance was still his father's, he was developing a style that was markedly his own.

In 1940 Joe Jr., a twenty-five-year-old student at Harvard Law School, shared his father's isolationist views and bitterness toward FDR. As a Massachusetts delegate to the Democratic National Convention the young man opposed a third term for the incumbent. The Roosevelt forces mercilessly beat on him to change his vote. But in this fiery baptism in national politics Joe stood firm. When the roll call ticked off the delegates' devotion to the president, he defiantly called out a protest vote for James A. Farley.[57]

After Pearl Harbor the Kennedys shed their isolationism and went to war. Young Joe became a navy pilot; Jack finally convinced the navy that he was serviceable despite a football injury to his back. He was given a desk job in Washington but used his father's influence to get transferred to PT boats. Even the ambassador wired Roosevelt that he wanted an assignment; the request was not granted.

Kathleen Kennedy returned to London to work in a Red Cross canteen and there fell in love with Billy Cavendish, Marquess of Hartington, son of the tenth Duke of Devonshire. The Cavendishes were among England's richest landholders. Their 180,000 acres included the estates of Chatsworth House, Hardwick Hall, Bolton Abbey, Compton Place, and Lismore Castle in Ireland. They were also militantly Protestant. The first Duke of Devonshire had withdrawn from the Privy Council of King Charles II in protest against Catholic influence, and the present duke was grand master of the Freemasons.

Kathleen went ahead with marriage despite her parents' protests. The wedding took place in May 1944 at the Chelsea Registry Office. Joe Jr., then stationed in England, stood by his sister during the family crisis and gave the bride away. The bridegroom wore the uniform of the Coldstream Guards. Kathleen, as the future Duchess of Devonshire, could expect one day to be first lady in waiting to the queen and mistress of the royal robes; the devout Rose could expect to be mother-in-law to the ranking Mason in the world. A London correspondent wrote, "One of England's oldest and loftiest family trees swayed perceptibly." Rose, in Boston, said she was "too sick to discuss the marriage."[58]

The young couple lived together for a little more than a month. Cavendish went into combat in France and on September 10, while leading an infantry patrol, was killed in action.

His death came three weeks after young Joe Kennedy died while performing a daring mission designed to destroy enemy submarine pens on the Belgian coast. Although eligible for rotation home, he had volunteered to fly a Liberator bomber loaded with 22,000 pounds of high explosives. The plan was for the pilot and copilot to parachute to safety when their plane neared the Channel coast, and for other planes to guide the Liberator to its target by remote control. Before reaching the bailout point Joe's plane suddenly exploded.

Within four years tragedy struck again. Flying to a reunion with her father on the Riviera, Kathleen's plane crashed into the Ardèche mountains. In the village of Privas, halfway between Lyons and Marseilles, Joseph Kennedy identified the body of his daughter.

"The thing about Kathleen and Joe was their tremendous vitality," Jack was to say. "Everything was moving in their direction . . . for someone who is living at their peak, then to get cut off—that's the shock."[59]

The untimely passing of Joe and Kathleen, marked by the family to lead their generation, was to move the younger Kennedys into an emotional overdrive. "The boys," said a friend in 1957, "are trying to live up to the image of Joe as they remember him. . . . The girls feel the same obligation to emulate Kathleen."[60]

AT WAR'S END, IF Jack had taken inventory he would have found that he had been trained for no profession; he was a war hero in peacetime, the savior of the crew of PT-109 after it had been rammed by a Japanese destroyer; his health was bad; he thought he might like to try his hand at newspaper reporting, but found it too passive; he had no interest in running his father's financial empire; yet neither did he have money worries or the necessity to administer his patrimony, since Joe Kennedy's office on New York's Park Avenue even took care of paying his personal bills.

The problem of what to do was solved for him in 1946 when Grandfather Honey Fitz's old nemesis, James Michael Curley, decided to give up his seat in the House of Representatives and try to become again mayor of Boston. Whether running for Congress was his idea or his father's is confused by contradictory quotations. "I got Jack into politics, I was the one," said the father. "I told him Joe was dead and that it was therefore his responsibility to run for Congress. He didn't want to. . . . But I told him he had to." Jack agreed: "It was like being drafted. My father wanted his eldest son in politics. 'Wanted' isn't the right word. He demanded it." But later, when he was a presidential contender and the ambassador was being sidelined for the duration, Jack explained, "I wanted to run and was glad I could."[61]

The Eleventh Congressional District was overwhelmingly Democratic. It included East Boston, Boston's North End and West End, Cambridge, Charlestown, and parts of Brighton and Somerville. The population was made up of Irish Americans, Italian Americans, and thirty-three other groups that were once connected by hyphens. It was Bunker Hill, Harvard University, and some of the worst slums in the city. The district also contained the former strongholds of P. J. Kennedy and John F. Fitzgerald. When Curley heard that a candidate bore both names, he said, "He doesn't even need to campaign. He can go to Washington now and forget the primary and election."[62]

Kennedys took nothing for granted. Friends came from Pittsburgh and San Francisco to work for Jack. Harvard students pitched in. Twenty-one-year-old Bobby, recently a seaman on the destroyer *Joseph P. Kennedy Jr.*, was put in charge of three East Cambridge wards. The Kennedy workers, according to Dave Powers, wore Eisenhower jackets on primary day—to remind voters that, besides a WAC major, Jack was the only veteran in the race. There was little chance they would forget: the district had been saturated with John Hersey's *Reader's Digest* account of Kennedy's heroics. Neither effort nor money was spared. "Jokesters around the State House took to wearing twenty-dollar bills in their lapels as 'Kennedy campaign buttons.'"[63] Jack received nearly as many votes as his eight primary opponents combined; the general election was a formality. Kennedy became the Bay State's youngest congressman in over half a century—in fact, since his own grandfather was elected to the same seat in 1894.

It was the year of a new order in politics, 1946. In California another young naval veteran, Richard Nixon, unexpectedly won a seat in Congress; Henry Cabot Lodge, back from army service, regained his place in the Senate; a marine named Joe McCarthy ended the La Follette dynasty in Wisconsin. The Republicans, under the leadership of Robert A. Taft, captured Congress for the first time in sixteen years. And twenty-nine-year-old John F. Kennedy began a career that had been reserved for his elder brother, now dead, and for which he felt he was not equipped.

THE YOUNG CONGRESSMAN, WHO moved into a house in Georgetown with his sister Eunice, had an orderly, analytical mind (*Why England Slept*), a high order of physical courage (his wartime experiences), stamina, and an attractive personality (his campaign for Congress). Columnist James Reston wrote, "The effect he has on women voters is almost naughty."[64] But he did not have a political philosophy or a body of experience to prepare him to serve a disadvantaged urban district. He was Choate, Harvard, Palm Beach. He was socially secure enough to arrive at a formal dinner at Perle Mesta's wearing brown loafers; financially secure enough to deliver a check to the archbishop for $1 million and not have the fare to pay the cabby.

The liberal-labor establishment of the Truman administration and the ethnic politicians who ran his state party found him enigmatic. He was elected because he was Joe Kennedy's son and Honey Fitz's grandson; since he owed nothing to the pols, this made him suspect in their eyes. Moreover, they had never liked his father in the first place. ("Drink bourbon," Harry Truman is alleged to have said. "Every time you drink Scotch you make Joe Kennedy richer!")[65]

While Jack voted the straight Fair Deal line, as his constituency required, the liberals questioned the depth of his convictions. He in turn told a *Saturday Evening Post* writer, "I'd be very happy to tell them I'm not a liberal at all. . . . I never joined the Americans for Democratic Action or American Veterans Committee. I'm not comfortable with these people."[66]

His attendance record was poor. He didn't have the herding instinct expected in a new House member. After two years in Congress he began making speeches in all parts of Massachusetts. He didn't yet know what higher officer he was seeking. All he knew was that he was in a hurry and could not wait for seniority to catch up to ambition.

The opportunity presented itself in 1952, when Henry Cabot Lodge Jr. came up for reelection. Kennedy may not have earned the nomination, but nobody else wanted it. The senator was formidable. Wrote Ralph Blagden in the *Reporter:* "It is difficult to see how Lodge deserves retirement."[67] Joe Kennedy urged his son to oppose Lodge. "When you've beaten him, you've beaten the best."[68] The Lodges were in the midst of a half-century love affair with the Boston Irish. The elder Senator Lodge had been the first Brahmin politician to recognize their growing power; he and his grandson had acted accordingly. Said Joe Kennedy, with disgust, "All I ever heard when I was growing up in Boston was how Lodge's grandfather had helped to put the stained glass windows into the Gate of Heaven Church in South Boston and they were still talking about these same stained glass windows in 1952."[69]

Lodge was met by a solid phalanx of Kennedys that would have pleased a Clausewitz:

—Father, lavish with advice, contacts, and money. One letter of solicitation began: "Believe it or not, Jack Kennedy needs money." But nobody took it seriously. The powerful Boston *Post* broke with its Republican tradition to endorse Jack; it was later revealed that Joe Kennedy had made a postelection loan of a half million dollars to the paper.[70]

—Brother Bobby, now a graduate of Harvard and the University of Virginia Law School, gave up his job with the Justice Department to become Jack's campaign manager. "Let Jack be charming to them," he said.[71] Bobby, without complaint, would be the hatchet man. (Younger brother Teddy was then serving an army hitch in Germany.)

—The Kennedy women. Mother Rose and sisters Eunice, Pat, and Jean introduced tea as a political weapon: 8,600 cups were consumed at one reception, and receptions were held in every corner of the state. "It was those damn teas that licked me," Lodge was reported to have said.[72] Ethel, Bobby's wife, made a speech in Fall River, then drove to Boston and had a baby. "When Archbishop Cushing baptized the baby . . . just before the election," said a Lodge aide, "that cut our hearts out."[73]

—Even ghosts of Kennedys past. A campaign tabloid featured a photograph of Joe Jr. captioned, "John Fulfills Dream of Brother Joe Who Met Death in the Sky over the English Channel."[74]

JACK KENNEDY TOLD AUDIENCES that "my grandfather, the late John F. Fitzgerald, ran for the United States Senate thirty-six years ago against my opponent's grandfather, Henry Cabot Lodge, and he lost by only 30,000 votes in an election where women were not allowed to vote. I hope that by impressing the female electorate that I can more than take up the slack."[75] He did. Kennedy won by over 70,000 votes. "At last," said Rose Fitzgerald Kennedy, "the Fitzgeralds have evened the score with the Lodges!"[76]

Joseph Patrick III, born and christened at propitious times during his uncle Jack's successful campaign for the Senate in 1952, was the first male of a new generation of Kennedys. Ethel Kennedy had given birth to a girl, Kathleen Harrington, the year before. She would eventually have eleven children—two, appropriately, on the Fourth of July—and, like her mother-in-law, would institute an index card system to keep track of their illnesses, vaccinations, and shots.

Slim, athletic, with brown eyes and sun-bleached hair, Ethel had no trouble adapting to the Kennedy clan. She too was from a large and wealthy Catholic family. Her father, George Skakel, was a self-made millionaire who started as a railroad man, became a traffic expert in coal, and went on to control the Great Lakes Carbon Corporation, one of the largest privately owned companies in the United States.

Ethel had been Jean Kennedy's roommate at Manhattanville College of the Sacred Heart. She further prepped for life as a Kennedy by writing her senior thesis on *Why England Slept* and working in Jack's first congressional campaign in 1946. She became known, in the Kennedy circle, as a fierce touch football player, even when pregnant; mistress of Hickory Hill, which abounded with pets (including a favorite sea lion), and the "only treehouse in the world that was designed by an architect"; a firm believer in the "method" school of living—whether it meant singing to Marian Anderson or spraying a member of European royalty from head to foot with an aerosol can of shaving cream. In the opinion of one writer, Ethel is an "authentic American primitive—vivid, informal, artless, positive, happy and spontaneous."[77]

Very different was the shy, wide-eyed beauty whom Jack Kennedy was secretly courting during his 1952 senatorial campaign. Jacqueline Bouvier was descended on her father's side from a French soldier who fought at Yorktown, and on her mother's side distantly from the Lees of Virginia and Maryland. Arthur Krock remembered her father, John Vernon Bouvier III, a New York stockbroker, as "one of the most famously attractive men" who ever lived.[78] A society reporter in East Hampton thought "that he much resembles one of those handsome Egyptians you see careening along in their Rolls-Royce cars in Cairo, in the land of the Nile!"[79] He was known at Yale as "the Black Orchid." Jacqueline's mother, Janet Lee, was the child of a conservative New York banker, president of the Central Savings Bank, who gave his daughter a duplex apartment on Park Avenue when she was married in 1928.

Twelve years later, "with a hint of scandal in the air," they were divorced.[80] Jacqueline was then eleven and her sister Lee was seven. Their Catholic father never remarried. But in 1942 their mother, an Episcopalian, became the wife of thrice-wed Hugh D. Auchincloss, a Washington stockbroker, whose winter estate in Virginia was called Merrywood and whose summer estate in Newport was called Hammersmith Farm. Auchincloss had three children, and would have two more with Jacqueline's mother. "It is a tribute to my mother," thought the future First Lady, "that though our family is steps and halfs, we don't feel like it. We are very close."[81]

Jacqueline attended exclusive girls' schools—Chapin in New York, Holton Arms in Washington, and Miss Porter's School in Farmington, Connecticut, where she kept her own horse. She summered in East Hampton (with her father) and in Newport (with her stepfather). When she formally entered society, Hearst columnist Cholly Knickerbocker dubbed her "Queen Deb of the Year." She was then a student at Vassar. Later she spent her junior year at the Sorbonne. She won *Vogue* magazine's Prix de Paris, having submitted an essay titled "People I Wish I Had Known." (They were Diaghilev, Oscar Wilde, and Baudelaire.) She finished her college education close to home at George Washington University.

She then became "Inquiring Camera Girl" for the *Washington Times-Herald*. For $42.50 a week she asked such posers as: What do you think of wrestling as a sport for women? Would you like to crash high society? Do a candidate's looks influence your vote? What do you think of psychoanalysis? "Psychoanalysis is not natively American. It was brought in by foreigners and has never added one bit to this country's peace of mind." She also went to Capitol Hill to find out what the solons thought of Senate page boys. Richard M. Nixon: "I would predict that some future statesman will come from the ranks of the page corps." John F. Kennedy: "I've often thought that the country might be better off if we Senators and the pages traded jobs."[82] Her biggest scoop came when she waited outside a Washington public school to interview the ten- and eleven-year-old nieces of president-elect Eisenhower. The story appeared on the front page, and the indignant mother called Jacqueline's editor to complain that her children's privacy had been invaded.

Congressman Kennedy's courtship of the Inquiring Camera Girl was a casual affair. He was away campaigning most of the time. Now and then he would call from some roadside pay phone "with a great clinking of coins." There were no love letters, just one postcard, "Wish you were here. Jack." When he proposed, the new senator said that he had decided to marry her a year before. "How *big* of you!" she replied.[83] The engagement was finally announced in June 1953. It had been planned for an earlier date but was postponed so that the *Saturday Evening Post* could put out an article on Jack titled, "The Senate's Gay Young Bachelor." They had a Newport wedding in September.

The new world of the Kennedys presented problems for a young woman whose sport was fox hunting—"it makes me feel clean and anonymous"—rather than touch football. When she tried the latter, she broke an ankle. "Everybody tells the story as though the Kennedys roughed up a young bride," she said. "But it wasn't that way at all. I was running happily along by myself near the sideline when I slipped and fell. There wasn't a Kennedy within yards." Thus ended Jacqueline Kennedy's career as a football player.[84]

There was also the problem of Joseph P. Kennedy. Early in her married life Jacqueline was late for lunch, a hitherto unpardonable sin in the patriarch's house. He started to needle her. But she cut him short, turning his slang and moralistic tales on him: "You ought to write a series of grandfather stories for children like The Duck with Moxie and The Donkey Who Couldn't Find His Way Out of a Telephone Booth."[85] Everyone waited for an explosion—instead Joe Kennedy broke out laughing. The bride had won her place in the dynasty. Later she would do watercolors especially for her father-in-law, such as one titled "You Can't Take It With You, Dad's Got It All." The family's judgment of Jacqueline was summed up by Bobby: "She's poetic, whimsical, provocative, independent, and yet very feminine. Jackie has always kept her own identity and been different. That's important in a woman. What husband wants to come home at night and talk to another version of himself? Jack knows she'll never greet him with 'What's new in Laos?'"[86]

Two Kennedys were present when the 83rd Congress convened in January 1953. Besides the new senator from Massachusetts, there was a new associate counsel of the Senate Permanent Investigations Subcommittee, Robert Francis Kennedy.

"Bobby is more direct than Jack. He resembles me much more than any of the other children," thought their father. "He hates the same way I do," Joe later added.[87] Unlike Jack, who tended to view issues as an intricate variety of grays, there was in his brother a tendency to see life in contrasting blacks and whites. Jack had a cool grace; Bobby was emotional, sometimes explosive. The two Kennedys shared a preoccupation with power. But since Bobby lacked Jack's finesse, it was more apparent in him. Here was a young man who had moved far and fast in the cause of his brother. And he moved with a straight arm. Ye those who knew him best said he also had an appealing shyness, his mother's deep religious convictions, and a sensitivity to family, friends, and associates.

By the time Bobby joined the McCarthy staff the Wisconsin senator had already added an "ism" to the language. Three years before, in Wheeling, West Virginia, he had announced the number of "known Communists" in the State Department. The association with McCarthyism did not seem to concern Bobby. The senator was known and liked by the Kennedys. The ambassador had contributed to his campaign for reelection; Pat had dated him; Bobby had invited him to speak at the University of Virginia. When, after six months, Bobby resigned from the McCarthy Committee, it was not because of a disagreement with the chairman but because of a personality clash with chief counsel Roy Cohn.

He then went to work for the Hoover Commission, which was proposing government reorganization, and of which Joe Kennedy was a member. Bobby found the work dull. Within eight months he was back on the McCarthy Committee as minority counsel to Democratic Senators McClellan, Jackson, and Symington. In this capacity he wrote the Army-McCarthy report, finding fault with both sides. But when the Watkins Committee voted to condemn McCarthy, Bobby was fishing in the Pacific Northwest. Jack was also absent, in the hospital having back surgery. He was one of two senators who had not voted on the McCarthy censure. "I was rather in ill grace personally to be around hollering about what McCarthy had done in 1952 or 1951 when my brother had been on the staff in 1953," the senator told James MacGregor Burns. "That is really the guts of the matter."[88]

AFTER BEING CLOSE TO death, Jack Kennedy slowly began to recover, and while his back was mending, he started writing another book. The idea came to him while reading about how Senator John Quincy Adams had voted for Jefferson's embargo against the dictates of his own party. Why not a series of essays on political courage as displayed by American legislators? His list included Senators Daniel Webster (for supporting Clay's compromise between North and South), Edmund Ross (for voting against the impeachment of Andrew Johnson), George Norris (for backing Al Smith for president), and Robert Taft (for opposing the Nuremberg trials). *Profiles in Courage* was an instant success. Critic Alfred Kazin felt the book reminded him "of those little anecdotes from the lives of great men that are found in *Reader's Digest,* Sunday supplements, and the journal of the American Legion."[89] Kennedy was surprised that some questioned his authorship. "The book isn't so good that it has to be ghosted," he said.[90] But book won the Pulitzer Prize. "I was on the Pulitzer board," said the New York *Times* columnist Arthur Krock, "and I worked as hard as I could to get him that prize."[91]

In *Profiles in Courage* Jack Kennedy wrote, "Few, if any, face the same dread finality of decision that confronts a Senator facing an important call of the roll . . . when that roll is called he cannot hide, he cannot equivocate, he cannot delay."[92] Along with his failure to face the dread finality of the McCarthy issue, the handsome senator-author had to listen to innumerable word plays (including Eleanor Roosevelt's) about "showing less profile and more courage." The Washington Gridiron Club—to the tune of "Clementine"—serenaded him with:

> Where were you, John—where were you, John,
> When the Senate censored Joe?

Jack Kennedy did cast one vote during his first term in the Senate that could have qualified him for a place in a revised edition of *Profiles in Courage.* This was on the St. Lawrence Seaway. Feeling that its passage was of overriding national importance, he voted against the narrower interests of the Port of Boston and his state. In 1960 he considered it the most difficult decision he had ever made. "It was the turning point," said his assistant, Ted Sorensen, "between Jack as a Massachusetts senator and a national statesman."[93]

BETWEEN 1953 AND 1956 the Kennedy family circle was increased by three as Eunice, Pat, and Jean were married.

Joe Kennedy paid daughter Eunice his highest compliment—she "has more drive than Jack or even Bobby," he said.[94] While all the girls were deeply involved in philanthropic and civic chores, Eunice was least inclined to choose the garden club variety. Once she spent a month inside a women's reformatory observing prison conditions. She was then executive secretary to the National Conference on Juvenile Delinquency and shared a Washington house with her bachelor congressman brother.

Eunice and Jack had the same mannerisms, even the same habit of stabbing the air with the index finger of the left hand; the same rapid-fire delivery, the same Boston accent, the same intellectual approach. Sargent Shriver said they were even subject to the same ailments. The man Eunice married was from the Catholic branch of an old Maryland family. His parents were both Shrivers—second cousins—and maternal Grandfather Shriver had been a state senator, as well as roommate during a brief seminary period of a Baltimore youth named James Gibbons. (Cardinal Gibbons was to be Sargent Shriver's godfather.) Sarge's father, at one time a vice president of the Baltimore Trust Company, was heavily hit by the stock market crash, causing the son to work while at Yale—as editor of the profit-making student newspaper—though he was still able to spend several college summers in Europe. As with the Kennedys, exposure to the European conflict turned young Shriver into an isolationist, but he too promptly enlisted as a submariner when the United States entered the war.

Returning from navy duty, the ruggedly handsome young veteran first joined a Wall Street law firm, found the work distasteful, then got a job with *Newsweek,* which his biographer felt was "slipping from under him" when Eunice introduced him to her father.[95] The chemistry was right. Joe liked the young man's competitive drive, frankness, religious convictions, and perhaps his prospects as a son-in-law. He gave him a job with the Merchandise Mart. After a six-year courtship, Eunice Kennedy, thirty-one, and Sargent Shriver, thirty-seven, were married by Cardinal Spellman at St. Patrick's Cathedral in 1953. The groom's mother wasn't overly impressed by her son's famous in-laws. "We're nicer than the Kennedys," she said. "We've been here since the 1600s."[96]

Three years later St. Patrick's was the scene of another Kennedy wedding. Jack's favorite sister, Jean, the youngest, quietest, and least political, married Stephen E. Smith. After college she had tried working among juvenile delinquents with Eunice in Chicago but felt herself emotionally unsuited for it and joined the Christophers, a Catholic organization dedicated to fighting Communism and raising moral standards. Her husband was a grandson of

William E. Cleary, a Brooklyn congressman who opposed Prohibition and supported river and harbor improvements.[97] "Old Bill" also founded a sizable tugboat business, Cleary Brothers, for which Steve Smith worked after graduating from Georgetown University and serving as an air force officer. "My real job," he said, "was to see that the captains weren't drunk and to get the coal loaded."[98]

"He is handsome enough," wrote Tom Wicker of the *New York Times*, "for one to imagine him dashing onto a Broadway stage in flannels, shouting 'Tennis anyone?'"[99] Yet behind his fashion-plate dress, shy manner, and clipped, rapid, barely audible speech there lurked a "nerveless bandit." Jack, Bobby, and Ted would become deeply indebted to their brother-in-law's skill at running their campaigns. Eventually he also supervised the Kennedy fortune. But Smith wished it understood: "My family had money before the Kennedys had money."[100]

Commenting on Jean's husband, Murray Kempton wrote in the *New Republic*, "For he is very like a Kennedy, even to the family intonations; and, since he gives the impression of having too much character to imitate an in-law, we may explain him as another example of the tendency of sisters in large families to marry young men who remind them of their brothers."[101] Eunice, in a corollary to Kempton's Law, lifted a champagne glass at her wedding reception in a toast to her new husband: "I searched all my life for someone like my father," she said, "and Sarge came closest."[102]

Nobody, however, could have mistaken Pat's husband for a Kennedy. When actor Peter Lawford was first presented to his future father-in-law he was wearing a blue blazer, white trousers, loafers, and bright red socks. "Mr. Kennedy," Lawford reported, "couldn't seem to take his eyes from the socks."[103] Peter was the only son of Lieutenant General Sir Sydney and Lady Lawford. For years he had been under contract to Metro-Goldwyn-Mayer and had appeared in a long string of mediocre films, playing such parts as Elizabeth Taylor's boyfriend in *Julia Misbehaves*. But at age thirty he had outgrown the college-boy roles and his career was foundering. His major claim to fame was as part of Frank Sinatra's "Rat Pack," among whose members he was known as "Charley the Seal." Pat and Peter were married in 1954, after he converted to Catholicism. Said Lady Lawford, "I wasn't too happy about Peter marrying into the Kennedy family." Her view was apparently shared by Joe Kennedy, who told her son, "Peter, if there's anything I think I'd hate as a son-in-law, it's an actor; and if there's anything I think I'd hate worse than an actor as a son-in-law, it's an English actor."[104] The marriage lasted eleven years.

FOR TED SORENSEN THE turning point between Jack Kennedy as a Massachusetts senator and as a national figure came with the vote on the St.
Lawrence Seaway, but to the more casual observer the turning point was the
1956 Democratic Convention. When Kennedy rose to place Adlai Stevenson's name in nomination for the presidency it was the first time that most
Americans had seen the handsome young senator. And when Stevenson
then threw the vice presidential nomination up for grabs, there was an immediate groundswell of support for Kennedy.

Stevenson's decision caught the convention off guard; the Kennedys
had only overnight to round up votes. "I'll never forget Bobby Kennedy
during the balloting," said Quentin Burdick of North Dakota. "Standing in
front of our delegation with tears in his eyes, he pleaded for our support."[105]
Even Peter Lawford was pressed into service, having connections in the
Nevada delegation. On the third ballot Kennedy climbed to within thirty-
eight votes of the prize, but then his vote total froze and Estes Kefauver
was nominated. Calm, smiling, Jack Kennedy climbed to the rostrum and
asked that the nomination be made by acclamation. The millions who had
watched the cliff-hanging drama on television now applauded a good loser.

The defeat in 1956 had an unusual effect on Kennedy. It dispelled the
curious belief that he was merely a shadowy substitute for his dead brother.
As he told Bob Considine in 1957, "Joe was the star of our family. He did
everything better than the rest of us. If he had lived he would have gone on
in politics and he would have been elected to the House and to the Senate as
I was. And, like me, he would have gone for the vice-presidential nomination at the 1956 convention, but, unlike me, he wouldn't have been beaten.
Joe would have won the nomination." Jack paused and smiled. "And then
he and Stevenson would have been beaten by Eisenhower, and today Joe's
political career would be in shambles and he would be trying to pick up the
pieces."[106]

By June of 1957, Jack Kennedy had become the most sought-after speaker
on the Democratic Party circuit, with appearances in nineteen states. A
fellow senator noted, "When you see a senator doing much speaking outside
his own state, it means one of two things. He needs the money or he's got
his eye on higher office. And Jack doesn't need the money."[107] Joseph Alsop
casually said to him in the summer of 1958, "Of course, the vice-presidential
nomination will be yours for the asking next time." Jack replied with a grin,
"Let's not talk so much about vice. I'm against vice, in all forms."[108]

The presidency was a far-fetched goal for a very young man and a Catholic. Yet even beyond this was the fuzzy outline of something seemingly more preposterous. As early as 1957, Harold Martin wrote in the *Saturday Evening Post:*

> Fervent admirers of the Kennedys profess to see in their rise to national prominence the flowering of another great political family, such as the Adamses, the Lodges and the La Follettes. They confidently look forward to the day when Jack [then forty] will be in the White House, Bobby [then thirty-two] will serve in the Cabinet as Attorney General, and Teddy [then twenty-five] will be the senator from Massachusetts.[109]

As Kennedys and their in-laws left homes in Boston, New York, Washington, Los Angeles, Chicago, and Palm Beach to join the family crusade for the presidency, Hubert Humphrey shook his head sadly. He felt like an independent merchant running against a chain store, he said.

Bobby, who had created a national reputation of his own as the counsel for the McClellan Rackets Committee, became his brother's campaign manager. Steve Smith came to Washington in January 1959 to open Jack's headquarters. He would be office manager, logistical expert, and administrator of finances and personnel. Ted, most amiable of the family, was put in charge of corralling delegates in the Western states. Sarge Shriver, now president of the Chicago Board of Education, ran two districts in the Wisconsin primary. Even the widow of Honey Fitz, the candidate's ninety-five-year-old grandmother, spoke by telephone from Boston to a dinner meeting in West Virginia.

But what role for Joe? An insider put the cost of the 1960 nomination drive at $1,150,000—and it can be assumed that most of it came from the family fortune.[110] Jack, with his uncanny ability to turn a political liability into an asset, told a New York audience that he had received the following wire from his father: "Dear Jack: Don't buy one vote more than necessary. I'll be damned if I'll pay for a landslide."[111] Joe would also use his contacts among old guard New York leaders. But the decision was made to keep the controversial ambassador under wraps. As an often-repeated couplet of the day went:

> Jack and Bob will run the show,
> While Ted's in charge of hiding Joe.

The show was masterfully run. Humorist Art Hoppe wrote that when a coffee machine in Kennedy headquarters went dry for three and a half minutes, "It was the first time in the memory of most observers that any machine remotely connected with Senator Kennedy's campaign for the Presidency had failed to function at peak efficiency."[112] The combination of Jack's attractiveness and Bobby's toughness—"a sort of sweet-and-sour brother act," said one politician—rolled to an easy first-ballot nomination.

"Of course, I'm voting for Nixon," was the caption of a *New Yorker* cartoon, "but I can't help wishing I could see what Jackie would do with the White House." Reporters speculated over whether the beautiful wife, a creature of haute couture and the jet set, would be a political liability. Twenty Iowa housewives signed a letter to the *New York Times* saying, "We have better-looking floor mops" than Jacqueline's bouffant coiffure. She was uneasy with the strange characters who surrounded her husband. Politics was the intruder in her home. Jack was always off campaigning; half of Caroline's first words (Daddy, airplane, car, shoe, hat, and thank you) had something to do with motion. Yet as her brother-in-law clearly perceived, Jacqueline Kennedy was a political asset. "We came out of that Los Angeles convention looking like a hard, tough family juggernaut," said Bobby, "but in her few gentle low-key TV appearances, Jackie softened that image and put the spotlight back where it belonged—on Jack and his family."[113]

The Kennedy strategy was to reconstitute FDR's winning formula—the coalition of urban politics, machines, Catholics, Jews, and other minority groups, while relying on vice-presidential candidate Lyndon Johnson to hold on to the once solid Democratic South. The Kennedys, thought a veteran Democrat, were taking a calculated risk. "They were going to talk about religion. They were the ones who brought up the religious issue and kept it alive. It wasn't the Republicans."[114] Bobby Kennedy, opening of a headquarters in Cincinnati: "Did they ask my brother Joe whether he was a Catholic before he was shot down?"[115] The major breakthrough with the black vote came after Sargent Shriver convinced the candidate that he should offer his sympathy to the wife of Martin Luther King, the jailed civil rights leader.

Nixon's attempt to brand his opponent as less mature was shattered by their first televised debate. Millions of viewers agreed that Jack Kennedy looked marvelous and sounded experienced. As Nixon's private pollster reported, "Kennedy . . . started the campaign as the less well-known candidate and with many of his adherents wondering about his maturity. He has done a good job [in the TV debates] of dissipating the immaturity label and . . . has succeeded in creating a victory psychology."[116]

The election was decided by two-tenths of 1 percent of the vote. Joe Kennedy had not paid for a landslide. As the returns came into the Kennedy compound at Hyannis Port, Jacqueline said to her husband, "Oh, Bunny, you're President now!"[117]

A PRESIDENT IN A family brings inevitable change. Shortly after the election Joe Kennedy determined that his children would go sailing. Jack declined. The patriarch replied, "I don't think the President should have to go if he doesn't want to."[118] Joe Kennedy had been a major influence in his sons' career decisions: Jack running for Congress, although the young man may have been eager to have the decision forced on him; Bobby going to work for the McCarthy Committee, which Jack opposed; Jack's decision to run against Lodge in 1952. Now he would again guide his flock into an unprecedented decision.

Another president, Woodrow Wilson, had once rejected his own brother as a postmaster after a "struggle," he said, "against affection and temptation."[119] But there was never a doubt that Robert F. Kennedy would be a part of the administration of John F. Kennedy. The question was, in what job? Father insisted that it should be attorney general, and Jack reluctantly agreed. When Bobby hesitated, Jack said, "We'll announce it in a whisper at midnight so no one will notice it." Later Jack told the Alfalfa Club, "I can't see that it's wrong to give him a little legal experience before he goes out to practice law." Bobby didn't think this was funny.[120]

The appointment drew an immediate outcry from those with accumulated complaints against the tough campaign manager. However, as columnist Robert Ruark pointed out, "A lot of people don't like Bobby, but nobody has to love an Attorney General." More serious were the objections of the legal profession. Wrote Yale law professor Alexander Bickel, "On the record, Robert F. Kennedy is not fit for the office."[121] Yet he was confirmed by the Senate with only one dissenting vote. At thirty-five Bob Kennedy became the second youngest attorney general in history—the youngest since thirty-three-year-old Richard Rush was appointed by James Madison in 1814.

Lawyers soon had to revise their estimates of the new attorney general. Despite (or perhaps because of) his inexperience, Bobby picked top aides of rare distinction. Judged Columbia University law professor William L. Cary, "I can say truthfully that no Attorney General assembled a group of assistants of such extraordinarily first-rate quality since Francis Biddle."[122] There were significant successes, notably in civil rights and fighting crime, as well as some failures, such as in civil liberties. But after two and a half years Washington correspondent Joseph Kraft concluded, "Justice has emerged as the most yeasty of all the Departments in the Administration."[123]

Bobby's role in his brother's administration ranged far beyond the confines of the Justice Department. He served as Jack's lightning rod, drawing attacks that would otherwise have been directed at the president; as an inner ear, listening to rumblings that tend to be filtered out before they reach the White House; as trusted adviser, flying to Indonesia to help settle the dispute over West New Guinea and to Brazil to discuss that country's economic crisis; as comforter when the Bay of Pigs invasion turned into a fiasco. Observing Bobby in action, Anthony Lewis of the *New York Times* concluded, "Certainly there has never been an Attorney General like him."[124]

Nor had there been a presidential brother-in-law like Sargent Shriver. Late in the 1960 campaign Jack suggested creating a Peace Corps, almost as an afterthought, and when he became president he put Shriver in charge of nurturing the idea. The founding director later liked to say that since "everybody concerned" was convinced the project would fail, Jack appointed him—reasoning "it would be easier to fire a relative than a friend."[125] He had been president of the Chicago branch of the Catholic Interracial Council and was a devout adherent of the liberal wing of the Church, in the tradition of his godfather, Cardinal Gibbons. The Peace Corps would be the ideal vehicle for his social commitment, and his Jimmy Stewart handsomeness appealed to the program's young recruits.

"IT'S TED'S TURN NOW," Joe Kennedy reportedly told his elder sons. "Whatever he wants, I'm going to see that he gets it."[126] What Ted wanted in 1962 was Jack's old seat in the U.S. Senate.

Though such lofty ambition on the part of a thirty-year-old was regarded as the height of political presumption, the president of the United States and the attorney general of the United States reluctantly agreed. It was Joe Kennedy's last great decision in making his sons the most elevated family triumvirate in American history.

The youngest son hardly had impressive credentials. He had been asked to leave Harvard at eighteen when it was discovered that he had induced another student to take a Spanish examination for him. He then entered the army as a private, and two years later returned to Harvard and graduated. He was also a graduate of the University of Virginia Law School and had served a short time as an assistant district attorney of Suffolk County.

John F. Kennedy (1917–1963) and Family
Left to right: Jacqueline Bouvier Kennedy, John F. Kennedy, Jr.,
President Kennedy, and Caroline Kennedy

Rose liked to tell audiences that "Teddy was the first American boy to receive his first Holy Communion from the Pope and I thought that with such a start he would become a priest or maybe a bishop but then one night he met a beautiful blonde and that was the end of that."[127] Teddy met Joan Bennett, the willowy, hazel-eyed daughter of a New York advertising executive, when he dedicated a gymnasium the family had given to Manhattanville College. Joan, a student there, decided to pass up the ceremony; she was a pianist, with little interest in gymnasia. However, a friend convinced her that she had better attend the Kennedy tea "because if they miss you, you'll get demerits and you might be campused."[128] Teddy had no trouble spotting the young woman who had spent a college summer modeling for television commercials. Cardinal Spellman married them the next year, 1958, during a ceremony in which the bride and groom were wired for sound movies.

The delegates to the Massachusetts Democratic Convention met in Springfield in 1962 to decide whether they would give their senatorial endorsement to Ted or to state Attorney General Edward McCormack. Years later Ted recalled the contest: "I thought I was reasonably well prepared because I had three or four advantages. I'd worked hard to acquire a brother who happened to be President, another who happened to be attorney general, a number of post office and other patronage appointments that happened to be available to dispense, and, of course, a dad who happened to have deep pockets." The Kennedy administration in Washington officially proclaimed its neutrality, but, as JFK put it, "We'd rather be Ted than Ed."[129]

Ted won the convention endorsement. Ed said he would win the primary on "the anti-*chutzpah* vote," but Ted defeated Ed by a two-to-one margin.[130] In round three, the general election, Ted faced George Lodge, son of the Henry Cabot Lodge who had lost to Jack Kennedy in 1952 and great-grandson of the Henry Cabot Lodge who had defeated Honey Fitz in 1916. Ted's campaign manager was brother-in-law Steve Smith, who now directed the Kennedy financial empire after brief service as a New Frontiersman with the State Department. Sensing an easy victory, Smith canceled many thousands of dollars' worth of television time. It was the sort of nervy judgment that the Kennedys respect—if it proves correct. Only George Lodge thought he had a chance. George was wrong.

"When the Kennedy administration becomes hereditary," wrote Malcolm Muggeridge for London's *New Statesman*, "the title of the heir, equivalent to our Prince of Wales, will presumably be the Senator for Massachusetts."[131] So a new Kennedy senator arrived in Washington, and in his first major address, before the Women's National Press Club, Teddy said: "I was down at the White House this afternoon with suggestions for the State of the Union address, but all I got from him was 'Are you still using that greasy kid stuff on your hair?'"[132]

IN EARLY 1963 THE *New York Times* reported, "Within the last six weeks, several magazines have appeared on the newsstands *without* cover pictures of Mrs. Kennedy." This was a respite, not a trend. The semilurid magazines fanned the public's curiosity. "Jacqueline Kennedy—America's Newest Star. What You Should Know about Her Fears" (*Photoplay*); "Another Baby for Jackie. The Wonderful News All America Is Waiting For" (*Movie-TV Secrets*); "The Secret They're Keeping from Caroline Kennedy" (*Motion Picture*)—the "secret" was that she is a celebrity. The president's wife said, "I think that people must be as sick of hearing about us . . . as I am."[133] Her thinking was wishful.

The public's fascination with the Kennedys was understandable. They were fascinating. The First Lady gave glittering musicales, wore shimmering gowns, renovated the White House, spoke perfect French to De Gaulle and Spanish to a group of farmers who gathered in a Venezuelan barnyard. Now she was seen water-skiing on the Riviera, now at her Virginia retreat in the hunt country, now touring India or the Greek isles. The old Eleanor Roosevelt joke was reactivated: "Good night, Mrs. Kennedy, wherever you are."[134] And the president, according to his friend Benjamin Bradlee of *Newsweek*, "could eat ten bowls of specially prepared fish chowder without succumbing to either indigestion or embarrassment, and though he smoked only rarely, he could chain-smoke three cigars when the spirit moved him. His ability to devour the written word was legendary, and he could unwrap presents faster than a five-year-old."[135]

It was generally taken for granted that Jack would be reelected in 1964 (though the Kennedys took nothing for granted, and Steve Smith, who had been designated by the family as the president's campaign manager, was already at work). In the closing hours of Jack Kennedy's first year in office, his father talked of him to a reporter. "I know nothing can happen to him," said Joe. "I've stood by his deathbed four times. . . . When you've been through something like that back, and the Pacific, what can hurt you?"[136]

On November 22, 1963, John F. Kennedy, the youngest elected president of the United States, was murdered in Dallas.

THERE WERE INTERNATIONAL SHOCK waves caused by the senselessness of the act, its brutality and suddenness; because a life of such promise now would be unfulfilled; because of the impact this young man of cool grace had already made on his world in the two years, ten months, and two days of his presidency.

His record in office included confirmation of a test ban treaty and a Trade Expansion Act, but at death his legislative program was in disarray. The president was keenly aware of the thinness of his electoral mandate; he felt hampered by the generational difference between himself and the legislative leaders. He had never been one of them; he didn't speak their language, which was primarily of the rural South and Midwest.

He reached his highest and lowest points in the handling of foreign policy. He gambled on overthrowing Castro by force, didn't commit the force necessary to succeed, and failed. But when Khrushchev moved missiles into Cuba he took the necessary steps to convince the Soviet Union that he would risk war to defend his nation's vital interests. The missiles were removed. "He assured his place in history by that single act," thought British Prime Minister Macmillan.[137] Yet on his death the Atlantic Alliance was decaying at the edges, and his Alliance for Progress in Latin America was more dream than reality.

John F. Kennedy was complex and paradoxical. Of robust elegance, he delighted in the biography of a little-known nineteenth-century English politician, in adolescent sports, in the polished style of Charles de Gaulle, in Ian Fleming's sex-and-intrigue James Bond stories. He felt operas should be performed in their original languages, and listened to the records of Chubby Checker. He enjoyed the company of a Schlesinger and a Sinatra, Robert Frost and Oleg Cassini. He was immersed in the statistics of government, and could tell Peter Lawford about the box-office receipts for the gangster film, *Ocean's Eleven*, in Manchester, England.

He was a politician—the only profession he had ever really practiced—who hated verbosity and pomposity. When William Attwood suggested during the 1960 campaign that he should "wave his arms the way other politicians did and give people a chance to get the cheers out of their throat," Kennedy borrowed a pencil (he was saving his voice for the day's speeches) and wrote, "I always swore one thing I'd never do is—" and he drew a picture of a man with his arms in the air.[138] He had a wry and irreverent wit, such as every campaign manual warns candidates against, yet he never lost an election.

SHE WAS "THE GIRL who has everything including the President of the United States," according to her secretary.[139] Jackie had been the third youngest First Lady; now, suddenly, she was the youngest presidential widow. Was there anything in her background to prepare the world for her majesty at her husband's grave? "She refused to be cheated of her right to this most terrible moment of her life," thought Katherine Anne Porter, "this long torment of farewell and relinquishment, of her wish to be conscious of every moment of her suffering: and this endurance did not fail her to the very end, and beyond."[140] Her job now would be to raise two small children and guard her husband in history. As celebrant of John F. Kennedy's memory she displayed a rare gift for the symbolic. She chose a grave site high up on a Virginia hillside overlooking the nation's capital and placed there an eternal light that flickers at night over the sleeping city. To the Kennedy crest she added a presidential motif—a fist clutching arrows, framed in olive branches.

If anything happened to me, Bobby would take my place.
—JOHN F. KENNEDY

BY EARLY SUMMER OF 1964 Bobby was finally emerging from the tragedy of Dallas. "There isn't that hollow look in the eyes," said a New York politician, "and the talk just doesn't turn automatically back to his brother the way it did a little while ago."[141] His own loss had been compounded by his highly developed tribal sense of family. Joe was incapacitated by a stroke. Joe Jr. was dead. Jack was dead. And Ted, flying in an Aero-commander to the Massachusetts Democratic Convention on June 19, 1964, crashed into an apple orchard. His administrative assistant and the pilot were killed. But Indiana senator Birch Bayh pulled Kennedy from the wreckage, his back broken. There would be five painful, immobile months before he returned to the Senate.

For Bobby there was the political problem of what to do. "I don't want to become a retired elder statesman at thirty-eight."[142] Ted's election as senator from Massachusetts locked him out of the state with which the family was most closely identified. So Robert Kennedy, who slept in Virginia, worked in Washington, and voted in Massachusetts, became the Democratic nominee for U.S. senator from New York. It was a marriage of convenience. New

York was a Democratic state with a Republican governor and two Republican senators. The party leadership was shattered from years of internal feuding. "They don't give a damn where Bobby lives," said a Kennedy confidant, "they want to win."[143] So the state party without a winner and the winner without a state were wed.

Bobby's campaign, as had been Jack's and Teddy's, became a call to arms for the entire Kennedy family. Steve Smith was again the campaign manager. (He was now being jokingly referred to as "Bobby Kennedy's Bobby Kennedy.")[144] Ethel, seven months pregnant with her ninth child, greeted voters in Brooklyn at the corner of Fulton and Pearl streets, and later gave three teas a week at her Long Island home. Her three eldest sons, ages twelve, ten, and nine, marched the entire length of the Columbus Day parade—from Forty-Fourth Street to Eighty-Sixth Street—wearing gigantic "Kennedy for Senator" buttons. Jacqueline appeared at the opening of her brother-in-law's headquarters. Nine volunteers, poring over transportation schedules and speaking requests, routed Eunice Shriver, Pat Lawford, and Jean Smith around the state. But the star was Rose Kennedy. On some days she appeared in both New York for Bobby and in Massachusetts for Teddy, running for reelection, using an all-purpose speech, merely changing the name to fit the occasion. A Kennedy aide recalls that it went something like this:

> The presidential days were cut short. Jack's enthusiasm, liveliness, ability, and faith are no longer with us. But he has bequeathed to us a wonderful legacy of purpose and of courage. Now we have (Bob/ Ted) to whom he entrusted his most ardent thoughts and ideals for which he worked so hard.

"Carpetbagger"—a word in little circulation since Reconstruction— became the leading issue in 1964's most interesting political contest. Senator Kenneth Keating, the Republican incumbent, reminded voters, "Why, there are people who have been standing in line at the World's Fair longer than Bobby has been living in New York."[145] Kennedy reminded voters that he spent his early years in the state, and made a sentimental journey to his childhood home in Riverdale, accompanied by three-year-old John F. Kennedy Jr.

But it was not the move to New York that bothered many New Yorkers so much as what was behind the move. As the *Times* said on September 2, Bobby is "a man in imperious pursuit of his star." Later, when the campaign became overheated, the newspaper dropped poetic niceties and announced,

Robert F. Kennedy (1925–1968) and Family
Back row: Mary Courtney Kennedy, then-New York Senator Bobby Kennedy,
Mary Kerry Kennedy, Ethel Skakel Kennedy holding Christopher Kennedy, Joseph
Kennedy. Front row: Kathleen Kennedy, Michael Kennedy, David Kennedy, and
Robert F. Kennedy, Jr. This photograph was taken in summer, 1964. On January 11,
1965, Mrs. Kennedy gave birth to her ninth child, Matthew Maxwell Taylor Kennedy.

"His intense ambition, supported by adroit political acumen and all the power in the Kennedy name and fortune that can be brought to bear, suggests that he is interested in the Senatorial office not for itself but as a means to an end."[146] Bobby replied, "Let's assume that I'm using this as a power base . . . let's just assume the worst. I can't go any place in 1968; we have a President. He's going to be a good President until 1972. . . . I'm going to have to do an outstanding job in the Senate if the people all over the country [are going to] demand that I be the [1972 presidential] candidate. So I don't see how New York suffers."[147]

What Bobby gave New York politics was star quality. At Jones Beach 10,000 bathers rushed forward to shake his hand; the helpless police told him that his presence would cause serious injuries, and he managed to make an escape. Arriving at the quiet little upstate town of Glens Falls at one in the morning, four hours behind schedule, he found that 4,000 persons (more than a fifth of the town's population) were waiting to greet him.

Bobby was elected by 800,000 votes. It was a solid victory, not a great victory: Lyndon Johnson defeated Barry Goldwater by 2.5 million votes in New York. During the campaign, Ted daily spoke to his brother from his hospital bed, giving advice and encouragement. The size of his victory was unprecedented. Jack had won a second Senate term by a record margin of 874,608; Ted's margin was 1,129,245 votes. Unlike Jack, who had largely relied on his own following, the youngest brother had worked constantly to solidify the regular party apparatus.[148]

At the opening ceremony of the Eighty-Ninth Congress, on January 4, 1965, Edward M. Kennedy of Massachusetts and Robert F. Kennedy of New York were sworn in as U.S. senators. Only once before, from 1800 to 1803, had two brothers served in the Senate at the same time. Never before had three brothers been senators.

With rising conflict in Vietnam and rising hostility to the war in the United States, Bobby's period of potential influence in the Senate would be short. He made an important speech on nuclear proliferation, helped start poverty programs in Bedford-Stuyvesant, Brooklyn, and worked for a more aggressive civil rights agenda. He gave a moving address at the University of Cape Town, South Africa: "Each time a man stands up for an ideal, or acts to improve the lot of others, or strikes out against injustice, he sends forth a tiny ripple of hope."

Bobby confronted a major decision on Vietnam. Should he challenge a president of his party who was expected to seek reelection? In continuous debate with his family and his entourage, he over-waited and was too late to lead the anti-war movement. Senator Eugene McCarthy of Minnesota got there first and forced Johnson into a narrow victory in the 1968 New Hampshire primary on March 12. Ted flew to Green Bay, Wisconsin, where McCarthy was campaigning, to propose some sort of Kennedy-McCarthy deal, which was instantly rejected. Bobby then entered the race on March 16 and was angrily denounced as an opportunist.

After President Johnson announced he would not run on March 31, Vice President Humphrey became the administration's candidate. But it was too late for him to enter the primaries. Bobby won primaries in Indiana (May 7) and Nebraska (May 14), though not in Oregon (May 28). If he could defeat McCarthy in California (June 4), he would be in the best position to challenge Humphrey at the August national convention in Chicago.

He did score a major victory in California. On election night, leaving a ballroom at the Ambassador Hotel where his supporters were celebrating, he was shot three times. On June 6, 1968, Robert F. Kennedy died in Los Angeles.

At the high requiem mass at Saint Patrick's Cathedral in New York on June 8, Ted spoke of how he wanted Bobby to be remembered:

> My brother need not be idealized, or enlarged in death beyond what he was in life; to be remembered simply as a good and decent man, who saw wrong and tried to right it, saw suffering and tried to heal it, saw war and tried to stop it. Those of us who loved him and who take him to his rest today, pray that what he was to us and what he wished for others will someday come to pass for all the world.

> If something happened to Bobby, Teddy would take his place.
> —JOHN F. KENNEDY

FOR THE LAST LIVING son of Joseph Kennedy Sr., this meant that it was now his responsibility to shepherd the family, and, if possible, to become president of the United States. Ted had three children and twenty-seven nieces and nephews.[149] He was the person to remind them of their heritage, sing songs and tell stories when they get together, always be available if needed. In each of his campaigns, he chose one of them to be his campaign manager: Bobby's children, Joe in 1976, Kathleen Kennedy Townsend in 1982, Max in 2000; his own children, Kara and Teddy, in 1988. When he had to decide when or if to seek the presidency, the family gathered to debate.

Caroline and John Jr. had need of their uncle's embrace after their mother died in 1994. Jackie was the bulwark against public intrusion into the young lives of the assassinated president's children. Caroline grew up to earn a law degree, marry a museum exhibit designer, have three children, write popular books on such subjects as the Bill of Rights and the right to privacy, compile anthologies on such subjects as her mother's favorite poems, and work for good causes such as raising private money for the New York City public school system.

She and Uncle Ted endorsed Barack Obama in the 2008 presidential primary when their support would be most helpful. Then Obama became president and made Hilary Clinton his secretary of state, meaning that the governor of New York would appoint someone to fill her Senate seat, and Caroline Kennedy, at fifty-one, decided "she'd upend a lifetime of privacy" for a "wildly unlikely bid to become a U.S. senator."[150] But the grubby side of politics was not designed for a novice. Rather than a campaign about public policy, the media was consumed with matters that she considered private. Her career as a politician lasted six weeks; she released a statement withdrawing from the race for "personal reasons." President Obama announced in 2013 that she was his choice to be U.S. ambassador to Japan, the dynasty's third ambassador, following Grandfather Joseph Kennedy Sr. and Aunt Jean Kennedy Smith. In 1993 Ted had wanted the embassy in Dublin for his sister, and President Clinton named her U.S. ambassador to Ireland, where she served into 1998, becoming a key player in the Northern Ireland peace process by successfully advocating a visa for Sinn Fein President Gerry Adams, which directly led to the IRA declaring a cease-fire in 1994.

Caroline's brother, John F. Kennedy Jr., also would earn a law degree and do good works, such as heading a group to provide opportunities for people with disabilities. But his primary business was starting a glossy magazine called *George*, whose first cover had model Cindy Crawford posing as George Washington in a powdered wig. John's life would end in the tragic and reckless manner that seems to be in the family's DNA. He bought a plane, Piper Saratoga II HP, and after fifty-three hours in the air—forty-three with an instructor, ten by himself—he set off on July 16, 1999, for his cousin Rory Kennedy's wedding with his wife and sister-in-law as passengers. The plane never arrived at the Martha's Vineyard Airport. On July 21 the bodies were recovered by navy divers. The National Transportation Safety Board determined that the probable cause of the crash was pilot error. John was thirty-eight. At a public memorial service, his Uncle Ted, paraphrasing William Butler Yeats, said of his dead nephew, "Like his father, he had every gift but length of years."

As a magazine publisher, John was accurate but not kind to two of Bobby's sons. In the September 1997 issue of *George*, devoted to temptation, he wrote that his first cousins, Michael LeMoyne Kennedy and Joseph P. Kennedy II, were "poster boys for bad behavior. . . .To whom much is given, much is expected, right?" The editorial was inspired by Michael having been accused of an affair with his children's underage babysitter and Joe being accused by his ex-wife of bullying her into an annulment. He claimed he was mentally incapable of entering into marriage at the time of their wedding. She was outraged by this unilateral canceling of a twelve-year marriage and wrote a book, *Shattered Faith: A Woman's Struggle to Stop the Catholic Church from Annulling Her Marriage.* Joe was a congressman planning to run for governor. His brother Michael was to run his campaign. Like their great-grandfather Honey Fitz's Toodles campaign of 1917, this was a campaign that was not to be.

Michael would soon die in a freak skiing accident in Aspen, Colorado, where the Kennedys gathered on New Year's Eve for the family's annual downhill football game. Warned by the ski patrol of dangerous conditions, still they formed two teams, and skiing fast and close, without poles, tossed a football through improvised goals as the sun sank. Michael hit a tree. "Michael, now is the time to fight. Don't leave us," pleaded Rory. She gave him mouth-to-mouth resuscitation, his blood staining her mouth. Michael had sought treatment for alcoholism and sex addiction. He was another Kennedy with a record of public service—founding a university in Angola, supplying heat to homeless shelters in Boston—who created his own destruction; his brother David, twenty-eight, would die of a cocaine overdose, alone in his room at the Brazilian Court Hotel, Palm Beach, Florida; his brother Robert, twenty-nine, was arrested in Rapid City, South Dakota, for heroin possession, entered a plea of guilty, and served 1,500 hours of community service. He subsequently built an eclectic career as an environmental activist.

Kathleen Kennedy Townsend, the eldest of Bobby and Ethel's children, was different enough to be known in the family as "Clean Kathleen" or "the Nun." She was the most dedicated of her siblings to pursuing a career in elective politics and was twice elected lieutenant governor of Maryland and then defeated as her party's candidate for governor. The Kennedy women seem more skilled at avoiding the addictions that plague their brothers. Rory, the youngest child, turned her social activism into producing and directing documentary films, including *Ghosts of Abu Ghraib* (2007) and *Last Days in Vietnam* (2014). She also did a film tribute to her mother, *Ethel*, which aired on HBO in 2012.

To continue the dynasty Massachusetts, Senator Kennedy hoped to convince his son Teddy to run for Congress. The Boston seat that had belonged to Jack Kennedy would be available in 1986 and Teddy would be at the constitutional minimum age of twenty-five. When twelve, Teddy had been diagnosed with bone cancer and his right leg had been surgically amputated. He was now thinking of doing graduate work at Yale in forestry and environmental studies. But his father was worried about him, and he agreed to do some breakfasts with potential contributors. The outcome was not what the senator had hoped, and instead the dynasty turned to Bobby's son Joe. Uncle Ted said, "That seat obviously has special meaning to our family. I'm proud of Joe, and I know his father would be proud of him, too."[151] Joseph Kennedy II had had a troubled youth, including a driving accident that permanently paralyzed a young woman. In 1979 he founded Citizens Energy to provide discount heating oil to low-income families. Joe was easily elected and served six terms, leaving Congress to run for governor, the plan that imploded. Teddy Jr., after his Yale degree and an alcohol treatment program in Hartford, became a lawyer in private practice. He also changed his mind about "the family business" and was elected to the Connecticut Senate.

His younger brother Patrick was already a politician. When a sophomore at Providence College, twelve days before his twenty-first birthday he announced his candidacy for a seat in the Rhode Island House of Representatives. He had hired a pollster to tell him the possibility of winning the $300-per-year job. The campaign cost about $30,000. His father spoke at house parties on Sunday afternoons on his way back to Washington, and a lot of Kennedys turned up on Election Day to help. Teddy won by 315 out of 2,333 votes cast to become the youngest Kennedy ever elected to office. The senator said, "None of the victories I have ever had in my political life has meant so much as this one tonight."[152]

Patrick was elected to Congress in 1994. When he left Congress in 2011, it was the first time since 1947 that there was no elected Kennedy in Washington. (Two years later another Kennedy would arrive to serve in Congress.) On May 4, 2006, Patrick crashed his green Mustang convertible into a barricade on Capitol Hill at 2:45 a.m. He had been drinking at a nearby bar, but claimed he was merely disoriented from prescription medications. He then admitted himself to a drug-rehabilitation facility at the Mayo Clinic, as he would do again in 2009. Patrick's history of drug addiction and alcoholism began when he was a seventeen-year-old high school senior. In a speech in Cleveland in 2008, he publicly acknowledged that he suffered from bipolar disorder. In Congress, Patrick was a chief sponsor of the Mental Health Parity Act, requiring most group health plans to provide coverage for the treatment of mental illnesses that is comparable to what they provide for physical illnesses. Out of Congress he cofounded One Mind for Research, an organization seeking to increase resources and efficiency in brain disorder research.

Kara, the third child of Ted and Joan Kennedy, died of a heart attack

Ted Kennedy, 1932–2009

after a workout at a health club in Washington. She had undergone aggressive treatment for lung cancer, and there was some media speculation that this had weakened her heart. She was fifty-one. Ted and Joan Kennedy separated in 1977. They announced plans to divorce in 1981, and the divorce was finalized in 1982. Joan had always felt a sense of inadequacy among the Kennedy women. Combined with the stress of Teddy losing a leg to cancer, the sometimes lonely life married to a politician, and rumors of a womanizing husband, Joan began drinking heavily. She was in and out of sanitaria.[153] Her children were first granted temporary guardianship, and she later agreed to a court-ordered guardianship.

The senator was also in a personal tailspin, his weight bordering on obesity, cheeks blotchy, involved in drunken and sexual incidents in Washington restaurants. Nor was his reputation helped by what happened on Easter weekend, 1991, at the family's Palm Beach estate. Kennedy went for a late-night visit to a local bar, getting his son Patrick and nephew William Kennedy Smith to accompany him. Smith was the son of Ted's favorite sister Jean and had just received his M.D. degree from Georgetown University. The two young men returned with women they had met and had sex. Smith said it was consensual; the woman, Patricia Bowman, said it was rape. The trial was a media frenzy, not equaled until the O.J. Simpson murder case several years later. All of the Kennedys were there for "an unprecedented display of solidarity." "We are a very close family," all of them said over and over again.[154] Smith was acquitted.

Kennedy's turnabout came after falling in love with Victoria Anne Reggie, a partner in a Washington law firm and a thirty-seven-year-old divorced mother of two children, ages five and eight. They were married on July 3, 1992. The media approached the pair with skepticism. The *Today* show asked the senator whether he had "got married for political reasons." He conceded that Vicki helped him politically. "But, you know, Vicki knows how much I love her. I have a sense about how much she loves me. My children know what it means for us to be together. Her children certainly have a sense of that. . . . And I think the people that see us together are coming to know that. And that's good enough for me."[155]

THE ULTIMATE QUESTION OF whether Ted Kennedy could become president of the United States was essentially resolved in the bizarre circumstances of July 18, 1969, sometime after eleven at night, when the senator turned right instead of left and drove his Oldsmobile into the water rather than onto an unlit humpbacked bridge that connected Chappaquiddick Island from Edgartown on Martha's Vineyard.

Kennedy was partying with a group of young women who had worked in Bobby's 1968 campaign. He left with twenty-eight-year-old Mary Jo Kopechne. After their car overturned, Kennedy said he didn't know how he escaped, but "repeatedly dove down to the car and tried to see if the passenger was still in the car." After swimming to shore, he made no effort to seek help, although he passed houses on the way back to his room at an inn. Nor did he mention the accident to other guests at breakfast. Early morning anglers spotted the wrecked car, and a scuba diver from the Edgartown Fire Department found the dead young woman.

A district court judge accepted Kennedy's "guilty of leaving the scene of an accident." The judge imposed a suspended sentence, saying, "He has already been and will continue to be punished far beyond anything this court can impose." In his confused account on TV, Kennedy admitted that failure to report the accident was "indefensible," then confessed to "all kinds of scrambled thoughts," including "whether some awful curse did actually hang over all the Kennedys."[156]

The year Ted chose to run for president, 1980, early polls showed him ahead of Jimmy Carter, the incumbent. Tip O'Neill, the House Speaker, warned his friend what polls don't say about what he called "the moral issue," and advised Kennedy not to run. Carter's attack ads never mentioned Chappaquiddick, yet there was no doubt what their oblique messages were referring to. In Chicago, where the Kennedys could always count on Mayor Daley, the issue cut deeply into his vote in conservative Catholic parishes. Even at home in New England, Kennedy on TV felt the need to say that "nothing is more difficult than when you know you alone are responsible for the loss of a young life." Kennedy's biographer, Adam Clymer, concluded, "Chappaquiddick, as the voters understood it, excluded him from the Presidency he might have won."[157] Carter lost decisively to Ronald Reagan.

Supporters and staff urged Kennedy to run again for president in 1984, and again to be a candidate in 1988. But after all the years in the Senate he was realizing that being a senator was a fully satisfying career. "I will run for reelection to the Senate. I know that this decision means that I may never be President. But the pursuit of the Presidency is not my life. Public service is."[158]

When Teddy Kennedy died in 2009 he was the second-most senior member of the Senate and the third-longest serving senator of all time. "Of all the Kennedys, the Senator is the only one who was and is a real Senate man," said Mike Mansfield, who had served with all three.[159] Backed by a remarkable staff, Ted saw more than 300 of his bills enacted into law. He had perfected the art of finding and collaborating with Republican senators with whom he otherwise had little in common. Utah's Orrin Hatch was a close ally on many health care–related measures. Arizona's John McCain recalled how Kennedy had been "a skillful, fair and generous partner." His cross-party deals irritated some liberal purists. But he clung to the adage "never let the perfect be the enemy of the good." *Time* called him "the Dogged Achiever," who had "amassed a titanic record of legislation affecting the lives of virtually every man, woman and child in the country."[160]

Ted was the last of the remarkable sons of Joseph P. Kennedy and Rose Fitzgerald Kennedy, but after the 2012 elections there would be a new Kennedy in Washington when Massachusetts elected Joseph P. Kennedy III to the U.S. House of Representatives. He was the son of Joseph P. Kennedy II, grandson of the New York senator. Those who were writing "last of the Kennedy" stories when Patrick left Congress in 2011 might at least have footnoted that a strength of the Kennedys as a dynasty is that there are so many of them.

EIGHTEEN

THE
Bush
DYNASTY

"Someone once said you don't understand politics until you've been
defeated—then all the mysteries become apparent."
—JOHN F. KENNEDY[1]

"I inherited all my father's enemies and half of his friends."
—GEORGE W. BUSH[2]

"I think the majority of Americans don't want to put up with the blue-
bloods—and I say it with all due respect, because I love the Bushes."
—SARAH PALIN[3]

T HE VOTES WERE IN, but the race was too close to call, and the
stakes too high. So the side that was (just barely) on the losing
end of the tally forced the issue before the state Supreme Court,
demanding a recount. "The closeness of the vote and the importance of the
office leaves us with no other choice but to reexamine the will of the people
to make sure it was reflected accurately by the results," said one party official.[4] And so unfolded the Bush dynasty's first foray into electoral politics—
Prescott Bush's 1950 Senate race in Connecticut.

In the days after voters cast their ballots, Bush, the Republican nominee, refused to concede to his opponent, William Benton, insisting that

he had a "real chance."[5] In many ways, it was surprising that Prescott had gotten this far. Compared to the old-guard families that had been there for generations, Bush was a relatively recent arrival in the state who had settled in Greenwich in a house paid for with help from his father-in-law so that he could commute to his job at Brown Brothers Harriman in Manhattan. Aside from his chairmanship of the Republican State Finance Committee and his role as mediator of the Greenwich town meeting, Prescott was a newcomer to politics.

The millionaire banker, Yale graduate, and president of the U.S. Golf Association campaigned as a moderate conservative, the connected outsider. He struck a populist note to push an antitax agenda. "The forgotten man," the average taxpayer, was footing the bill for a minority of underprivileged while the Truman administration and Connecticut's Democratic senator were driving up deficits. "We believe that thrift is still a virtue," Prescott concluded, "and should be encouraged, not sabotaged." He quoted Jefferson on public debt, but sounded more like Friedrich von Hayek when he said, "To preserve our independence we must not let our leaders load us with perpetual debt. We must make our choice between economy and liberty or profusion and servitude."[6]

The Benton-Bush race teetered on the edge of electoral chaos. There was no provision for a general recount. According to one reporter, "The complexities of Connecticut's election laws troubled the justices as much as the lawyers."[7] Sailing into this unknown territory meant that the state GOP had to contest the results of all 169 towns in Connecticut. The state Supreme Court dutifully took these petitions, one at a time, but after they threw out the first three challenges on "insufficient evidence," the Republicans reluctantly withdrew. Prescott quietly wrote a letter congratulating Benton, and privately wondered if he would ever make another attempt.

The fact that he did make another attempt, and another, set in motion a familial commitment to politics now into the fourth generation. The rise of the Bush dynasty is remarkable not just for its successes but also for its losses. When Prescott tried again for the Senate in 1952, he didn't even secure the nomination. It was a special election later that year that got him into the Senate. When his son, George H. W. Bush, ran for a Senate seat in Texas in 1964, the result was a resounding loss. This was followed by another one in 1970. His son, George W. Bush, failed in his bid for a seat in the House in 1978. The elder George fell short of the GOP presidential nomination in 1980, and lost after one term to Bill Clinton in 1992. His son,

Jeb Bush, who was a family favorite to carry the torch forward, lost the race to become Florida's governor in 1994.

This dynasty became a dynasty because of its ability to take a loss. Other potential dynasties might have left the battlefield. The Bushes inoculated themselves to this phenomenon. Each generation sought new territory. Prescott, son of a midwestern manufacturer, became a Connecticut banker. George H. W. moved to Texas to go into oil exploration. George W. didn't find real success in business until he owned a baseball team. Jeb moved to Florida and went into real estate.

The Bush family persistence is even more remarkable when one considers that it always had other options. Banking, oil, manufacturing, sports, real estate—they made fortunes in all of these arenas. At any point they could have retreated from electoral politics back to occupations where they had proved their mettle. But the family ethos, since Prescott, dictated that business success is for the sake of being in politics, never to be enjoyed merely for itself. That unwritten rule has given the Bushes security in knowing that their families will enjoy the trappings of wealth even while enjoying the trappings of political power. It has also contributed to the perception that the Bushes are insular elitists.

When Prescott was a senator, he was surprisingly outspoken in opposing increased salaries for those serving in Congress. Once, after stating his opposition to a salary increase, his Republican colleague from Connecticut, Senator William Purtell, asked him some pointed questions: "Would the Senator feel that one of the prerequisites for membership in the Congress should be either inherited or acquired wealth?" He then detailed struggles faced by some members of Congress in maintaining two homes—one in their district, the other in Washington—for their growing families. Prescott replied, "I would remind the Senator that such persons are not compelled by any requirements except their own preference to serve in the House. There is no compulsion for such persons to remain members of the House if they do not think the reward is satisfactory and they find themselves in positions of hardship."[8] The Bushes—Prescott, George H. W., George W., and Jeb—would ensure that they were well into economic comfort before entering politics.

Once raised high enough to meet this standard, Prescott's descendants have been forced to actively challenge the charge of elitism. This is difficult when the family carries such social markers as prep schools, Ivy League colleges, secret societies, golf clubs, and a summer compound on the Maine coast. The fight against the perception of privilege and entitlement helped transport George H. W. to Texas, when there was nothing wrong with New England, and it helped convince George W. to sever himself even more from his New England roots. It allows members of each successive generation to appear to be making it on their own, following their own paths, fashioning distinct identities, even with the full use of the family's extensive networks and wealth.

At the center of this creative tension is the dynasty's habit of denying that they are a dynasty at all. "We don't think that way," insisted George H. W. "We certainly don't see ourselves as a dynasty. *D* and *L*—those two words, dynasty and legacy—irritate me." George W., even after becoming president, echoed this sentiment, at times nearly verbatim: "There is no Bush dynasty, not now not ever." Jeb was more concise: "Dynasty schmynasty," he quipped while serving as governor of Florida, his brother running for president.

"We don't feel entitled to anything," said George H. W., by way of explaining why the family is not a dynasty. "We have nothing to pass on except our willingness to serve," adding, "We are not about exercising power." George W. insisted that "to talk about a political dynasty would be an act of conceit." According to Jeb, "It connotes something that was been kind of given to you, and it hasn't been. We have worked very hard to get to a point where we can serve people."[9]

That very aversion to the idea of a dynasty, when coupled with a sense of entitlement, privilege, and top-down guidance by a pater familias, is itself embedded in the family's experience. When George H. W. ran against Ralph Yarborough in Texas for a U.S. Senate seat, one of the most withering lines of attack centered on Bush's family connections. "Big ole Daddy . . . out to buy hisself a seat in the United States Senate," Yarborough taunted. "Let's show the world that old Senator Bush can't send Little Georgie down here to buy a Senate seat."[10] And George W. faced more of the same in his first bid for a House seat in 1978. His primary challenger called him "Junior" and said he was "riding his daddy's coattails." His Democratic opponent explained that the federal government was a mess "because of all those Yale fellas running the place."[11]

Being a Bush begets political problems for the other Bushes. While George W. had to contend with his father's preppie profile, Jeb has to contend with his brother's presidential decisions and falling approval ratings. Showing an awareness of this, George W. promised, at a closed-door meeting of donors, that he would stay off the campaign trail and out of sight

Senator Prescott Bush and Dorothy Walker Bush, center, with
their children, grandchildren, and in-laws in 1956
Left to right: TK
GEORGE BUSH PRESIDENTIAL LIBRARY

because, in the words of one attendee, "He basically said that [Jeb] is going
to have some issues with the name 'Bush' to contend with." Another donor
recalled George W. adding that "the country doesn't like dynasties," and
commenting, "People are going to say, 'Oh, here comes another Bush.'"[12]

PRESCOTT HAD ENJOYED A successful career in sales and was also successful in distancing himself from his father, Samuel P. Bush. The two
had grown distant after Prescott's service in the World War I; family lore
chalks this up to a bizarre misreading of a letter Prescott had sent from
Europe. The young artillery officer described how he had single-handedly
deflected an incoming artillery shell with his bolo knife, saving the lives of
General Foch, Sir Douglas Haig, and General Pershing, thus winning the
highest honors of France, Britain, and the United States. Prescott's mother

apparently missed the joke, and the local paper ran a front-page story on Prescott's heroism. The retraction and apology was a huge embarrassment for the Bushes of Columbus, Ohio. This contributed to a falling out between Prescott and his father that never really healed, and helped propel the son into new ventures far from home.

While rejecting the opportunity to work directly with his father, his father's influence came through indirectly, and especially through Skull and Bones. There may have been many reasons for Yale's secret society to tap Prescott, but the fact that Samuel ran Buckeye Steel for Frank Rockefeller, brother of John D. Rockefeller, and listed railroad baron E. H. Harriman as one of his clients prompted Prescott's selection. Percy Rockefeller, son of William, was part of the secret society, as was E. H. Harriman's son Roland. Prescott's membership was due to a mix of personal merit and family connections; among Bonesmen he could both take advantage of his family's position and display a measure of independence.

Prescott's first job put this dynamic on full display. He went to work for Wallace Simmons, a Bonesman, who founded a hardware company. Instead of managing manufacturing companies, as his father did, he went into sales. Instead of settling in Columbus, where his family had a firm social position, he struck out for St. Louis, newly married to Dorothy "Dottie" Walker, who was seven years his junior but several notches above him in social standing. Soon Prescott was hawking a diverse array of products—Keen Kutter tools, Klipper Kut ice skates, Krystal Klear lanters, Karpet King sweepers—that had little in common aside from how they abused conventional spelling. Among the many jobs he held in the first few years of his marriage, he did accept one offer from his father: Samuel asked him to move back to Columbus to help save a floor coverings business he had acquired. But the company flopped and was sold at a loss, and the attempt by Samuel and Prescott to salvage their relationship didn't fare much better.

In two years, he and Dottie lived in four cities. It was during their brief stay in Massachusetts that George Herbert Walker Bush was born. By the end of their second year of marriage, they were expecting their second child. Accepting an offer from US Rubber brought Prescott back to Connecticut, this time as a commuter from Greenwich to New York. This also brought him back into the Skull and Bones orbit.

Roland Harriman was working with his brother Averell in the family firm, Harriman Brothers & Co. The firm had at its helm Dottie's colorful and hard-driving father, George Herbert Walker. Prescott may have preferred to make his own way—the family lore suggests he was driven by this impulse—but the lure of so many stars aligning in lower Manhattan and the increased pressures of a growing family made a job offer from Harriman Brothers irresistible. He entered the firm, one of the largest on Wall Street, as a vice president. A few years later, after the stock market meltdown, Harriman got together with Bonesmen at Brown Brothers & Co. to engineer a merger that created one of Wall Street's largest investment banks.

Prescott remained with Harriman Brown Brothers for some forty years (stepping aside temporarily when he became a senator). He served on seventeen corporate boards, including CBS and Pan American Airways. When the stock market was weak during the depression, he made money as a broker, using his extensive list of contacts and his professional-level golf game to lure new business. His father-in-law retired in 1931, so he was no longer under anyone's shadow.

Prescott's commitment to public service was not inherited. His father had served briefly on the War Industries Board during the Great War and on Hoover's Committee for Unemployment Relief in the early years of the Great Depression, but his longest sustained service was to the game of golf and the founding of the Scioto Country Club. And his father-in- law was known as a Gatsby-type figure who encountered no feelings of guilt over his riches or yearnings for public service. He held that wealth was to be enjoyed in the form of mansions, yachts, and vacation homes, not dispatched to shore up one's family while pursuing a life of public service.

Prescott had briefly flirted with the idea of joining the clergy, which would have meant following in his grandfather's steps rather than in his father's. Surrounded by wealth and all its trappings, Prescott never felt comfortable with the ostentatious displays of his father-in-law, or the boisterous competitiveness of Wall Street. In addition, by 1950, Prescott had several reminders of his long-delayed call to service.

His son had jumped at the chance to serve in World War II just as he had in World War I. George H. W. Bush made his intentions clear before graduating from Phillips Academy, as had many of his classmates. Prescott was less than enthusiastic, but he remembered when he had been at Yale and with several classmates had joined the Connecticut National Guard, received training over the summer, and forming the Yale Battalion on their return. At the time, the U.S. Army was fighting irregulars along the Mexican border, and the newly minted Ivy League privates were hopeful they'd be called up. The president of Yale quietly quashed that idea. Prescott perfectly understood why his son was signing up.

Family tree is TO COME

George was forging his own path, and Prescott watched as he enrolled in flight school, was commissioned an ensign, and became, just days before turning nineteen, the youngest pilot in the U.S. Navy. He watched as George flew fifty-eight combat missions, was shot down, and received the Distinguished Flying Cross, three Air Medals, and, along with the rest of his unit, the Presidential Unit Citation. George was a bona fide war hero. He was also a husband, having married Barbara Pierce while home on leave in 1945. She was nineteen and dropped out of Smith to be his war bride. Her father was the president of McCall Corporation, the women's magazine publisher. The Bushes may have been a flyspeck higher on the social ladder.

DURING THE WAR, PRESCOTT helped raise millions for the National War Fund and the United Service Organizations. He was surrounded by colleagues whose public service he admired. Samuel F. Pryor, with whom he served on the Pan Am board, oversaw the construction of dozens of secret airbases in North Africa and Latin America. Another friend, Allen Dulles, was serving in a newly fashioned espionage outfit, the Office of Strategic Services, in the shady world of wartime Switzerland (here, Prescott played a supporting role by assisting with the secret transfer of funds). Among his partners at Brown Brothers Harriman, Averell Harriman was ambassador to the Soviet Union and Robert Lovett was to be the under secretary of state and then secretary of defense.

Prescott's path to service would be in elective politics, running for the Senate in 1950, thus setting in motion an unintentional dynasty. The *Washington Post* called the 1950 election season in Connecticut a "three-ring circus." The new politician enlisted the help of the Yale Whiffenpoofs—he sang second bass, belting out "I'll Raise the Deuce When I Get Loose in Town"—and the Brooklyn Symphony Orchestra, "an aggregation of musical zanies" who showed up "dressed in weird costumes—one man wears a dinner jacket and lace pantalettes." Prescott joined them on banjo. The *Post* editorialized, "Lots of people think this is an awful funny way for a former trustee of Yale to act in public."[13]

In the final days of the campaign, a Boston columnist wrote that Bush couldn't win because of his association with the Birth Control League, given Connecticut's large Catholic population. The Bush family labeled this a falsehood. In the family's mind, this serves as the first of many betrayals by the fourth estate.

Then too, there was the ugliness of internal GOP politics that challenged Prescott's carefully cultivated sense of decency and fair play. On a trip to Washington, Senator Owen Brewster briefed him on the Republicans' strategy of laying the ills of the world on Secretary of State Dean Acheson. "I don't think you can make that sort of case," sources recalled him saying, "How do you know that Acheson is entirely to blame? What proof do you have?" A veteran reporter remarked on how Bush was "an innocent in the great game of politics." Brewster assured him that they had the backing of Secretary of Defense Louis Johnson.[14] It is unlikely that this made Bush more comfortable. Acheson was a trustee of Yale. But Bush, Brewster, and Johnson were connected through Pan American Airways. Prescott's long campaign of cultivating connections, which had served him so well in business, was to place him in one awkward position after another when it came to politics.

The next election drove this home. Prescott ran again in 1952, but failed to secure the nomination. Later that year, however, he became the Republican nominee in a special election caused by the death of Senator Brien McMahon. His Democratic opponent was Congressman Abraham Ribicoff. If politics makes strange bedfellows, it can also make strange enemies. Averell Harriman, Prescott's longtime friend and business partner, paid a visit to the Connecticut Democratic convention to endorse Ribicoff and cut down Bush. This hurt. "Harriman made a speech calling for my defeat. Why did he do that?"[15] The two avoided speaking for more than a decade.

As part of an effort to draw a sharp contrast between the Republicans and Democrats on foreign policy, the GOP sent Joe McCarthy to Connecticut in early 1952, a move that struck fear into the hearts of moderate Republicans. Prescott was under intense pressure to appear with the senator; a failure to do so was tantamount, in the political climate of the time, to enlisting as a fellow traveler in the Communist cause. Prescott introduced McCarthy at a rally in Bridgeport's Memorial Hall. As he recalled, "I went out on the stage with my knees shaking," but gave McCarthy a warm welcome. When the cheering died down, he added, "I must say in all candor that some of us, while we admire his objectives in the fight against communism, we have very considerable reservations concerning the methods which he sometimes employs." The response was predictable: "The roof nearly blew off with boos and hisses and catcalls and cries of 'Throw him out!' 'Go back to Russia.'"[16]

On the floor of the Senate in 1954, Bush was one of the first Republicans to unequivocally denounce McCarthy: "Either you must follow Senator

McCarthy blindly, not daring to express any doubts or disagreements about any of his actions, or, in his eyes, you must be a communist, a communist sympathizer, or a fool who has been duped by the communist line."[17]

Prescott's stand on McCarthy came up in the 1992 presidential campaign debate when George H. W. Bush attacked Bill Clinton's antiwar activities and his trip to Moscow. Clinton responded, "When Joe McCarthy went around this country attacking people's patriotism, he was wrong. He was wrong. And a senator from Connecticut stood up to him named Prescott Bush. Your father was right to stand up to Joe McCarthy; you were wrong to attack my patriotism. I was opposed to the war but I loved my country."[18] This was a shrewd and disarming ploy. The son deeply admired his father, modeled his political persona after him, and had experienced the pang of not living up to his father's principles before. He gave no reply, but that particular line of attack on Clinton ceased.

Prescott's tenure in the Senate was one of quiet service and loyalty to his party. When he briefly took a spot in the national limelight as the chair of the GOP's 1956 Resolutions Committee, responsible for drafting the party's platform, a reporter's brief biography noted his performances with the Whiffenpoofs to make a point about his pragmatic politics: "Close harmony being a Republican specialty under President Eisenhower, the hottest close-harmony man at Yale . . . would seem to be an ideal choice for the convention job."[19] The most fraught section of this platform would be the plank on civil rights.

The Supreme Court had recently ruled in *Brown v. Board of Education*. The Democratic platform had a tepid statement on civil rights and racial integration that pleased no one. Prescott promised a stark contrast to the Democrats. He had long been a backer of the United Negro College Fund and, more recently, had cosponsored substantial bills that gave the federal government a direct role in protecting voting rights.[20] "We concur in the conclusion of the Supreme Court that its decision directing school desegregation should be accomplished with all deliberate speed locally thru federal District courts," read Bush's plank. However, the platform also spoke of "the complex and acutely emotional problems" that desegregation would create "in certain sections of the country." NAACP executive secretary Roy Wilkins weighed the GOP platform as merely "a thin shade better" than the Democrats.[21] Weighing Prescott's idealism and pragmatism, his pragmatism appeared to have prevailed.

Meanwhile, George H. W. Bush was following in his father's footsteps by not following them too closely. A Yale honors graduate and banker's son, he easily could have started his career at Brown Brothers Harriman or another Wall Street bank. Instead, like his father, he went into sales, and, like his father, he moved out of state, and then kept moving. Like Prescott, he followed his opportunities rather than his passion. He and Barbara settled in Midland, Texas, to seek a fortune in oil. This phase of his career is often painted as pioneering, with little to sustain this Yankee-bred couple among the tumbleweeds. But George and Barbara appeared in a 1951 photo spread in *Vogue* that detailed the lives of the surprisingly large number of couples settling in Midland from all corners of the country. "They have brought with them not only college educations, but a great working enthusiasm to build there, with time, what they want to build." They hailed from Princeton, Harvard, Yale, Dartmouth, Vassar, and Smith, but also from the University of Texas, the University of Kansas, and Arizona State. "To them," opined *Vogue*'s reporter, "everything is new, nothing static, and these are friendly, happy people, thinking seriously and responsibly, living with bright optimism." This optimism was easy to see reflected in Barbara Bush, "a tweedy girl with a deep staccato laugh."[22]

Prescott had proudly refused financial support from his father but welcomed it from his father-in-law. George H. W. avoided the appearance that Prescott was paying his way but took a great deal of help from his uncle and namesake, George Herbert Walker Jr. When he decided to strike out on his own, he and his partner raised $350,000 to form the Bush-Overbey Oil Development Company, and later joined with another entrepreneurial venture to form Zapata Petroleum. Prescott contributed $50,000 of the initial seed money; George Herbert Walker Jr. picked up most of the tab. This was not an industry with a low bar to entry. Being in oil required connections and investors willing to play the high-risk, high-reward game of poking holes in the ground to see if a fortune lay underneath. George H. W. worked extremely hard; Barbara made sacrifices as well. Still, his name created the opportunity.

Zapata made George H. W. a millionaire before forty, and once again he took a page from his father's book. His family was already secure, so that he could enter politics without having to wait until he was in his mid-fifties. He moved to Houston in 1958, where new oil wealth was encouraging the Republican Party in a state that had been solidly Democratic since Reconstruction. Like Prescott, he started by working within the party structure. Prescott had been Republican finance chairman in Connecticut; George H. W. served as chairman of the Harris County Republican Party, learning the lay of the land, increasing the size of his Rolodex, and establishing himself

Caption TK
Left to right: Neil Bush, George H. W. Bush, Jeb Bush, George W. Bush, and Marvin Bush
GEORGE BUSH PRESIDENTIAL LIBRARY

as a team player. He also used the position to attempt to build bridges with the far right of the party, at this point represented by the John Birch Society, a rabid anticommunist organization that still idolized McCarthy.

By the time he ran for Senate in 1964, his father had left public service for health reasons (he would go to his grave regretting the decision), and George H. W. was establishing his bona fides as an arch conservative. He called himself a "responsible conservative," but his positions were far right, his attacks centered on his opponent's liberalism, and political observers noted that he was moderate only in terms of temperament. "A slightly refined Goldwater Republican," columnists Rowland Evans and Robert Novak called him.[23] He was challenging Ralph Yarborough, a long-serving senator who was swimming against the tide of an increasingly conservative Texas electorate. Bush accepted the policies of Barry Goldwater early in the year, argued against the nuclear test ban treaty that had cleared the Senate, 80 to 19, and opposed the landmark 1964 Civil Rights Act, which he called "politically inspired" and "bad legislation in that it transcends the Constitution."[24] To a friend, he revealed the political side of this stance: "The civil rights issue can bring Yarborough to sure defeat."[25] At the same time, he was uncomfortable with the support his positions received from die-hard segregationists: "What shall I do?" he asked in a private letter. "How will I do it? I want to win but not at the expense of hurting a friend nor teaching my children a prejudice which I do not feel."[26]

Bush touted his war record and stopped wearing button-down shirts, deflecting charges of being a carpetbagger and profiting from foreign petroleum exploration (a cardinal sin in oil country), and by late October he had cut into Yarborough's commanding lead to the point where the race looked like a dead heat. Yet George H. W. Bush's first run for national office ended in defeat. Neither the opinion polls nor the candidate expected the African American vote to more than double: in 1960 about 105,000 African Americans voted in Texas; in 1964, the vote was up to 260,000, 95 percent for the Democrats.[27] The issue Bush thought was sure to bring Yarborough's defeat had instead ensured his victory.

Bush lamented his choices both publicly and privately: "I took some of the far right positions to get elected," he told his pastor, "I hope I never do it again. I regret it." In a public postmortem in the *National Review*, he encouraged Republicans to "re-package our philosophy, emphasize the positive, eliminate the negative, warn of the dangers of the left but do so without always questioning the patriotism of those who hold liberal views," adding that "conservatism can and will survive—it needs to be practical and positive."[28] When he ran for a congressional seat two years later, he put party funds in a black-owned bank, courted students at Texas Southern, a black college, by placing a party office nearby, and vowed "I will not attempt to appeal to the white backlash."[29]

George H. W. was fifteen years younger than Prescott had been when he made the leap from businessman to public servant. Being a U.S. representative looked like a good place to start. His district was urban and wealthy, his constituents were much like him in temperament and open to the practical, positive conservatism he'd advocated in the *National Review*. Unlike a statewide election, he didn't have to pander to rural voters, who would see him as a Yankee carpetbagger, no matter how much he tried to sound like a southern Bircher. George H. W. won with 57 percent of the vote in 1966, catching the attention of national Republican figures. Prescott suggested to the right people that this novice congressman be given a seat on the all-powerful Ways and Means Committee; two former presidents, Ford and Nixon, added their endorsements.

Representative Bush managed to reverse most of the principles he had assumed during his Goldwater-inspired 1964 campaign. He voted for the

1968 Civil Rights Act. He looked more and more like his father as he worked across the aisle, repudiated extremism, and supported access to birth control (so vehemently, in fact, that one of his colleagues started referring to him as "Rubbers"). His seat was so safe that he was willing to entertain tax increases and cuts to NASA that would directly affect his Houston constituents. Unlike his father, who served in Congress for eleven years without making a play for higher office, George H. W. became restless after just two years.

Was a vice presidential nomination possible in 1968? Prominent business friends and donors were urged to suggest that Bush was exactly what Nixon was looking for in a running mate. Nixon rebuffed the overtures, but was enough impressed by the ambitious congressman to ask him to again challenge Senator Yarborough in 1970. If Bush should lose after giving up a safe seat in the House, Nixon promised him a "soft landing."

This was a pivotal moment, a moment of high political risk, in George's career. Prescott, unsurprisingly, advised against the move. George went to see Lyndon Johnson, who told him the difference between being a representative and being a senator was "the difference between chicken salad and chicken shit." In the end, there wasn't going to be a Yarborough-Bush rematch in that Yarborough lost in the Democratic primary to conservative Lloyd Bentsen, who then convincingly defeated Bush. So George was out of a job, despondent, full of self-doubt. "I'm looking introvertedly and I don't like what I see," he told his supporters, "I must've done something wrong."[30]

His sons were also deeply affected by the defeat; reportedly, they both openly cried. They had participated in the campaign, with Jeb taking time out from Andover and George W. appearing on the campaign trail in his Texas Air National Guard flight jacket. The campaign mudslinging was nothing compared to what George H. W. had been through in his run against Yarborough, but the proud father had still faced the familiar charges: carpetbagger, elitist, not a true Texan, relying on father rather than on his own hard work. George W. and Jeb were old enough to realize that they too would have to overcome similar judgements. It must have seemed doubly unfair in that their feelings about the family's Yankee roots ran the gamut from indifferent to hostile.

Both had been raised in Texas, which right away gave them identities distinct from their father's. Yet when they were shipped off to Andover, they found themselves in the part of dad's long shadow they were least familiar with and least attracted to. George H. W. had captained the baseball and soccer teams, had been class president, and had an air about him that transcended the cliquishness of elite institutions. George W., who was perfectly happy back in Texas, did not excel at sports or academics and did not understand, or really want to understand, New England's unwritten rules. "Going to Andover was the hardest thing I did in my life, until I ran for president."[31] Jeb faced similar difficulties, "The signals that they sent were not subtle to people from outside the region." As their father struggled in Texas to distance himself from these New England roots, his sons struggled with being defined as boorish Texans by preppie New Englanders.

Jeb's Andover was starkly different from the place George W. had known. The elder brother, who graduated in 1964, was considered an anti-authoritarian troublemaker because he organized an unsanctioned stickball game (which possibly doubled as a way of lightly mocking his dad's seriousness about baseball). For Jeb, who was there at the height of the Vietnam War protests, students were "chaining themselves to the federal building in Boston. It was not a great time to be at that school. It was not a happy place."[32] George W. had his copy of Goldwater's *Conscience of a Conservative*, a gift from his father, who was running as a far-right candidate, and found in it much that appealed to him. Jeb joined the socialist club, objected to the war, and told his father he might register as a conscientious objector.

George W. turned to back-slapping humor and bonhomie to become a big man on campus in his own right. His experience was not so horrible as to convince him that he needed to retreat back to Texas after graduation. Rather, when asked by Andover's dean to list his top three college choices, he put down Yale, Yale, Yale. The dean thought it unlikely that he'd be admitted, but when George filled out his application, using both sides of a page to list all the relatives who were Yale alumni, and that included his grandfather, a U.S. Senator and a Yale trustee, a solid C average turned out to be good enough.[33]

The strategies that George W. had used at Andover were of limited use at Yale. The campus was embroiled in counterculture politics and Vietnam protests, and there was little room for a happy-go-lucky scion with mildly conservative views outside of the DKE fraternity. George W. was tapped for Skull and Bones, but never immersed himself in that secret society as his father and grandfather had. He drank, smoked, sneered, and bided his time until graduation, when he could fly fighter planes. "Being a pilot. That was all he ever talked about," recalled a Yale classmate. To a pointed query from an officer in the Texas Air National Guard, George replied, "I want to be a fighter pilot because my father was."[34]

Going a route his father had once chosen was sufficient for George.

What's more, the fighter pilot persona stuck with him, as did his self-assurance in his choice. When in 2003 he landed on the aircraft carrier *Abraham Lincoln* to declare the Iraq mission accomplished, there was no hiding the references to the father's World War II heroism, the attempt to link it to the father's war against Saddam Hussein, and the larger attempt to place the invasion of Iraq on the same moral high ground as the war fought by his father. George W. knew that this display would call attention to how he managed to avoid going to Vietnam; amazingly, he didn't seem to care. His own service was tightly linked to his father's, and he felt it was nothing to be ashamed of.

AFTER GEORGE H. W.'s second loss in trying to reach the Senate, Nixon did arrange a promised landing, but it was anything but soft. He would be U.S. representative to the rancorous United Nations in New York. As a novice in the realm of foreign relations, he sought a learning experience that might one day be useful. He would have to answer to Henry Kissinger, who, according to Deputy National Security Advisor Alexander Haig, asked, when informed of Bush's appointment, "Vat am I to do with this turkey?"[35] With Kissinger serving simultaneously as national security adviser and secretary of state, Bush's influence was going to be minimal. On a few critical issues, Kissinger kept him completely in the dark.

Then the chairmanship of the Republican National Committee became vacant in early 1973, and Bush got a chance to try to attend to the needs of his party, also a role of future usefulness. But he had to shelve his plans as the Watergate scandal turned him into chief apologist and damage control engineer for a soiled presidency. When the details of the scandal first came to light, Bush blamed Nixon's advisers and loyally soldiered on, ignoring that he ran a high risk of being dragged under by the crisis. Bush finally realized that Nixon had betrayed his office after the release of the "smoking gun" tape and asked him to resign at a cabinet meeting in a room full of Nixon loyalists. Nixon resigned two days later.

As Gerald Ford, now president, considered those who might be his vice president, George H. W. was a name under consideration. (Eventually he would turn to Nelson Rockefeller, who had not been close to Nixon and Watergate.) Bush was offered a plum European ambassadorship. He calculated its worth and asked instead for assignment in China. His time at the UN and his observations of Kissinger and Nixon had convinced him that the opening of China introduced boundless opportunities and would go even further toward establishing his foreign policy credentials. In addition, he would get out of Washington, a place that still had the stench of scandal.

According to historian Timothy Naftali, "No American politician had ever tried so hard to be vice president and failed."[36] This is especially remarkable because he was so perfectly suited to the role. He had proven repeatedly his loyal service to party and president while disregarding the cost to his own career. He had brains and ambition, but never strove to eclipse his colleagues or superiors. He was exactly what any president would want, but once again his ambition was thwarted.

Bush, the available man, next moved from China to the CIA. How he got there is in question. Most agreed that the office of the director of central intelligence was where political careers went to die, and this would be doubly true now as the agency was under intense scrutiny for previous activities such as assassination plots, domestic spying, and toppling foreign governments. Bush had left Washington in the wake of a scandal and returned to one that was still frothing. George and Barbara greeted the job offer with morose tears. As if to rub salt in their wounds, Senator Frank Church insisted, as a condition for confirmation, that Bush *not* be considered a candidate for vice president.

WHILE GEORGE WAS RAKING in political consolation prizes and jumping from post to post at the whim of his presidential patrons, George W. was jumping from job to job. Typically they were jobs his father's network helped him land; he referred to one as a "stupid coat and tie job."[37] He had stretches of unemployment, failed to get into law school at the University of Texas, and was drinking with increasingly serious consequences, including a drunk driving arrest while his teenage sister was in the car. "You have disappointed me," his father told him. Reflecting on this moment years later, George W. said, "When you love a person and he loves you, those are the harshest words someone can utter."[38]

George W. didn't tell his parents he was applying to Harvard Business School, and didn't tell him he'd been accepted. Instead, in 1973, according to one of the most often-told glimpses inside this very private family, he crashed his car into his parents' neighbors' garage door and drunkenly confronted his father with an invitation "to go mano a mano right here." Jeb intervened with the news that his big brother had been admitted to Harvard. George W. insisted that actually going to Harvard wasn't the point: "I just wanted to show that I could do it."³⁹ Then, armed with a Harvard MBA, he immediately traced a familiar path: In 1948, George H. W. had graduated from Yale and driven his red Studebaker to Midland, Texas (the car is now parked at his presidential library); in 1975, George W. drove a blue Cutlass to the same destination to go into the same business.

Like his father, he had no trouble raising investment capital to start an oil company. Unlike his father, he did not meet with success. George H. W. had painstakingly built a company after low-level experiences in several aspects of the industry. George W. tried a race to the top; oil exploration often involves a lot of luck, and George W. seemed to be banking on luck—not an unreasonable strategy, but one that failed this particular Bush.

George H. W.'s entry into politics was, like his father's, based on preliminary work within the party machinery and operated from a position of comfortable wealth. George W. jumped into the fray in 1978 without either. Midland's congressman was a Democrat who had fended off challengers for forty-three years in an increasingly Republican state. His retirement was a golden opportunity for a conservative Republican with the backing of the Bush family and its ever-growing network. George W., raised in Midland and Odessa, expected to be accepted as a Texan, but he wasn't. His Democratic opponent, State Senator Kent Hance, who advocated policies just as conservative as Bush's, never failed to remind audiences that while Bush was at Andover, Yale, and Harvard, he was at Texas Tech and the University of Texas, and he loved to tell the story about the cattle guard: A visitor asks a farmer for directions to town, and the farmer tells him to take a right at the cattle guard. The driver heads back before too long to ask what color uniform the cattle guard is wearing. "I got the poor fella straightened out on cattle guards," he concluded, "As he was leaving, I couldn't make out whether his license plates were from Massachusetts or Connecticut."⁴⁰

The two Bushes dealt with defeat in different ways. The father would become dour, blame himself and his own shortcomings, take stock of his policies and beliefs. The son hardly seemed affected. But something important had happened in his campaign: His father worked behind the scenes and dispatched young strategist Karl Rove to Midland; his mother was an effective manager of the list of friends; younger brother Neil was campaign co-manager; younger sister Doro performed with a tambourine on the campaign trail. The family had pulled together, and for the first time the spotlight was on him, not his father. In addition, he had a bride to campaign with him. In 1977 George W. Bush married Laura Lane Welch, of Midland.

Her father was a home builder, her mother was the bookkeeper. She had degrees in education from Southern Methodist and in library science from the University of Texas at Austin.

JEB'S CHOICES IN THE 1970s were more independent of Bush traditions and folkways. Central to this was Columba Garnica de Gallo, who became Columba Bush in 1974 when she was twenty and Jeb was twenty-one. He would later say that his life divides into "BC and AC—before Columba and after Columbia."[41] Trying to cope with culture shock at Andover, he took a class trip to Mexico and at seventeen met Columba, felt "lighting" at first glance, and returned determined to win her over despite the vast distances between them—geographic, social, cultural—as well as his parents' concern. He shook off the cynical stoner persona he had acquired and finished his bachelor's degree in two and a half years at the University of Texas. (Yale, he said, was something he never even considered.)

His father's connections helped Jeb get a job at Texas Commerce Bank. It wasn't Wall Street, but it was commerce and banking. His B.A. degree in Latin American studies and his fluency in Spanish put him in an excellent position when the bank opened a branch in Caracas, Venezuela, to handle the money being pumped out of the oil industry. He relocated with Columba and their two children, quickly establishing himself as a magnetic salesperson. He managed to convince Lady Bird Johnson, who was on the board of Texas Commerce, to visit Caracas, which got the American embassy to host a reception, which granted Jeb access to the country's business elite. He might have stayed longer except that his father was running for president, a family enterprise. "That's when I caught the bug," he recalled, "It was perhaps the most rewarding experience of my life."[42]

He was a natural for outreach and speeches about his father before Latino audiences, especially in Miami's Little Havana. "God, Jeb is doing fantastic," his father noticed. "He has such good judgement, good with people, great grasp of the issues."[43] The rest of the family lined up as well: The candidate's brother Johnny cochaired the finance committee; brother Prescott Jr. handled finances in Connecticut. His daughter Doro learned to type and take shorthand. His son Marvin canvassed in Iowa while taking time off from the University of Virginia, and his son Neil jumped into the fray in New Hampshire. Barbara took up her husband's offer to travel on her own and was largely responsible for her own schedule, carefully crafted from her long list of contacts that she had been building since George was at

Yale. The helpers extended far beyond the candidate's immediate family. A cousin compared the campaign office to a family reunion. The Bush-Walker clan seemed to fashion a team out of each family member's sense of competitiveness, with each one believing he or she can contribute more than their sibling, cousin, aunt, or uncle.

The candidate, however, had two overriding problems. His opponent, Ronald Reagan, was the generation's star personality in politics, and the voters were moving away from George's brand of moderate policies. Yet there were good reasons for Reagan to choose George as his running mate. Bush would temper the hard edges of the candidate's conservatism and bring a wealth of experience to the ticket—especially foreign policy experience. Bush had also proved during the scandal-plagued seventies that he could carry a president's water. Now in the Reagan White House, known for infighting and clashing egos, George stood as an oasis of loyalty. The vice presidency was a job that might lead to the presidency, but that would depend on how well Reagan did, and this was largely out of Bush's hands.

With the patriarch on ice, waiting his turn to run again for president, the family's center of activity shifted to the flurry that was Jeb Bush. He had campaigned extensively for his father in Florida. After the election, having worked without pay, Jeb was nearly broke. But having a vice president for a father didn't hurt, as he admitted. He entered the Miami real estate business on the invitation of a Cuban immigrant who had millions to spare and a new business to run. Bush quickly became his partner and soon could enter politics on his own terms. As chairman of Dade County's Republican Party, following his father's and grandfather's tradition, he showed he was willing to work the party apparatus at a relatively low level. He also insisted that he would plot a career without his father's help. "We have an unwritten rule about nepotism," he told a reporter.[44]

Fair enough, but the Bush family operates in other ways. George H. W. got elected on his own terms to the House, but then was propelled onto the stratospheric Ways and Means Committee through his father's influence. In Miami, Jeb got his father to come to Florida to help elect a Republican governor in 1986. Governor Martintez then appointed thirty-three-year-old Jeb to be Florida's secretary of commerce.

THE BUSH POLITICAL DYNASTY had been taking shape for thirty-eight years, and 1988 was likely to be George's last chance to become president. The election might be close. At one point he trailed Democrat Michael Du-

kakis by seventeen points. The Republican candidate's response was to give
free rein to strategist Lee Atwater's instincts to go deeply negative, with ads
attacking Dukakis's patriotism and stance on crime. Gone was the genteel
Bush family ethos, at least for a time.

The first Bush presidency oversaw the end of the Cold War and the dismantling of the Soviet Union. The president was pragmatic, moderate, and
restrained. He avoided bragging and bravado, even as the Berlin Wall came
down and his advisers were calling loudly for victory laps. He saw serious problems in the budget deficit that his predecessor had helped create,
and hoped he would be able to balance the budget by working closely with
congressional Democrats. The Gulf War might have been called unchar-
acteristic for him (Margaret Thatcher thought he was going "wobbly" by
not jumping into the fray), but he went about the planning methodically,
worked through the UN, avoided big risks, planned a military invasion that
worked, and then gave up his own private hope for a regime change when
the dangers that policy presented became clear.

He had accepted his party's nomination with what many Republicans
considered a pitch-perfect speech in which he declared, "Read my lips: No
new taxes." But in the fall of 1990, with a budget crisis and rising debt, the
president knew that taxes would have to be on the table. The budget deal
he worked out with the Democratic majority was unacceptable to Minority Whip Newt Gingrich, who led a revolt from the margins that quickly
spread to the party's mainstream. Ultimately, Bush received the support of
thirty-two House Republicans out of 168. A President, who had seen his
approval skyrocket to nearly 90 percent after the successful Gulf War of-
fensive in Kuwait, would have to watch it plummet as the nation suffered
an economic recession along with tax increases, rising unemployment, and
continued budget deficits. Bush, the forty-first man to be president of the
United States, lost his reelection bid to Bill Clinton. The dynasty's future
would have to depend on the political skills of his sons.

GEORGE W., TIRELESS DURING his father's 1988 campaign, still had to
confront his drinking problem if he was to take center stage. Some of the
pieces of sobriety were in place. He had been attending Bible study since
the mid-eighties and already thought of himself as born-again. He had an
ultimatum from Laura, and with his father's rise to the presidency came
opportunities, including the possibility of buying the Texas Rangers. (His

great-uncle Herb Walker had once owned the Mets.) The team was a be-loved Texas institution. As he told a local news program, "This job has very high visibility, which cures the political problem I'd have: What has the boy done?"[45] He quickly raised $75 million, despite no experience in running a professional sports team. His own contribution was $600,000, but since he put the deal together, he was handed a 10 percent share. So his $600,000 turned into $7.5 million overnight. He would ultimately rake in $15 million.

He was now a public figure and worthy of being a gubernatorial candidate. Suddenly a long-simmering family squabble burst into public view. Barbara sent a message to her son, first through aides, and then through reporters. "I'm hoping, having bought the Rangers, he'll get so involved that he won't do it." George W. did nothing to contain his resentment. Also using a reporter to get a message to mother: "Thank you very much. You've been giving me advice for forty-two years, most of which I haven't taken."[46] Barbara wanted that year's Bush candidate to be Jeb, but the younger son wasn't coming along as quickly as George W. He had a net worth far less than the Ranger windfall, a family that seemed to need him, and a wife who strongly preferred to stay out of the public eye.

THE SHOCK OF BUSH 41 losing the presidency, when it had once seemed so certain to continue to a second term, galvanized the Bushes and cleared the way for both Jeb and George to take their turns at keeping the family in politics. While Jeb started his race for governor of Florida methodically and with the family's full backing, even permission, George W., in Texas, was asked to back off, partly because his parents felt he would be deflecting funds from his brother, but also because they did not think he could beat Ann Richards, the sharp-tongued incumbent, who had told the 1988 Democratic National Convention that George H. W. Bush had been born "with a silver foot in his mouth." Florida Governor Lawton Chiles, whom Jeb would be challenging, was considered vulnerable. By November, however, polls in Texas and Florida showed movement in unexpected directions. On election night the family's predictions were inverted: Bush was the new governor of Texas, Chiles was reelected in Florida. George W. got on the phone with his father, who was distraught about Jeb's loss, and continued to lament about what terrible news this was until W. cut him off: "Why do you feel bad about Jeb? Why don't you feel good about me?"[47]

GEORGE HAD ACCOMPLISHED SOMETHING his father had twice failed to do--win a majority of the Texas vote--and was now in uncharted waters. Despite the wide array of political positions held by family members, no Bush had served as a governor. He was now the political standard-bearer for the dynasty (and now it really was a dynasty), and there was no familial reference point to guide him. He could be his own man.

In an interview with the *Houston Post*, he embraced evangelical Christianity. "Heaven is only open to those who accept Jesus Christ," he said.[48] His cousin John Ellis was compelled to comment, "I always laugh when people say George W. is saying this or that to appease the religious right. He *is* the religious right."[49] Even if his faith wasn't put on display for the sake of votes, it had that effect, and appealed to a segment of the Texas electorate that had grown tired of being ignored. It was also a clean break from the muted Episcopalian religiosity of his parents and grandparents. They didn't talk openly about faith because it wasn't *polite* to do so. George W.'s lack of qualms about bearing witness, and Jeb's conversion to Catholicism, added a new dimension to the Bush dynasty.

And yet he governed Texas much as his father might have. He reached across the aisle to work closely with Democrats and formed a real partnership with his Democratic lieutenant governor. He refused to take a hard line on immigration, even when it became clear that heated rhetoric was paying political dividends in California. He signed a law that guaranteed spots in public colleges and universities to students in the top tenth of any Texas high school graduating class—as a response to the courts' dismantling of affirmative action. He even proposed offsetting cuts in property taxes with increases in other taxes.

THE SECOND BUSH PRESIDENCY came down to 537 votes out of 6 million in Florida, the margin of victory in the final tally after the U.S. Supreme Court intervened in the 2000 Florida recount. In this extraordinary chapter in the story of this extraordinary dynasty, the growing vastness and influence of the Bush dynasty became apparent. Jeb was by now governor of Florida and had promised to deliver his state's twenty-five electoral votes to his older brother. Cousin John Ellis was on the election desk at *Fox News*, keeping W. informed of the see-saw in the vote count. As the issue moved to the courts, it was President Bush's former secretary of state, James A. Baker, who headed the legal team. And then there was the eerie historical

Caption TK
Credit tk

parallel: fifty years earlier, Prescott Bush had lost in a close election after a bid for a recount was stopped by the courts.

GEORGE W. BUSH TOOK a hard right turn into the White House. He had once told a reporter, "Don't underestimate what you can learn from a failed presidency," clearly referencing his father, and it appeared that the calculation was that what worked in the Austin statehouse would lead only to another one-term Bush presidency.[50] His economic policy was dedicated to a massive tax cut, and he bluntly told Congress he was not into negotiating. Even when he became a wartime president he continued to cut taxes, grandly adding to the federal deficit.

In a sense, however, the Bush 43 presidency began again on September 11, 2001, with him standing at Ground Zero, megaphone in his hand, telling the firefighters and police officers, "I can hear you. The rest of the world hears you. And the people who knocked these buildings down will hear all of us soon." At that moment, he was the most respected man in America, perhaps in the democratic world.

There is no more far-reaching aspect of the Bush presidencies' competing legacies than the two wars in Iraq. Bush 43's war undid much of the legacy of Bush 41's war—the undoing of Vietnam syndrome and the return of global respect for American military might. George W.'s war demonstrated the limits of American power, turned America's voters against overseas deployments, and emboldened America's enemies. As the rationale for going to war was repeatedly undermined by new information, it allowed public imagination to fixate on a truly awful contention that this war was really about a son trying to prove himself to his father. It should not have been a serious charge, yet George W. didn't help when he said things like "After all, this is the guy who tried to kill my dad," a reference to an assassination plot that was likely hatched in Saddam's Iraq.

JEB WAS FINALLY ELECTED governor of Florida in 1998, reelected in 2002. As governor, he was by most yardsticks more conservative than any of the Bushes. He relentlessly cut taxes, by $19 billion, and routinely vetoed new spending—to the tune of $2 billion. He added over a dozen new laws to expand the rights of gun owners, including the controversial "stand your ground" law. He stood fast against legal protections for gays and lesbians, ensured that vouchers were included in his education plan, dismantled affirmative action via executive order, and privatized Medicaid. His two positions that were a hair shirt for conservatives were immigration (he wanted a pathway to citizenship or permanent legal status for the undocumented) and education (he backed the Common Core state standards).

WHAT IS IN THE dynasty's future? There have been two Bush presidents. Will there be a third? A fourth? Beyond 2016, Jeb and Columba's son George Prescott (known as "P" in the family) works a political career in Texas; a lawyer and former public school teacher, he was elected Texas Land Commissioner in 2014, an obscure job that apparently is politically important in the state. He is a cofounder of Hispanic Republicans of Texas: by heritage, a Bush is eligible to become the first Hispanic president.

THE BUSHES STILL MUST confront "the curse of the presidential dynasty." Not all dynasties wish to include a president on their family tree. Most are content with senators and governors. But there have been six dynasties with presidents: Adams, Harrison, Roosevelt, and Bush, two; Taft and Kennedy, one. (Discount the Harrisons, to whom having a president was a semi-accident.) Each family with two set out to seek a third (or a fourth, given the two branches of the Roosevelts). In each family with one, a second sought the presidency. All failed. They failed because of the person or the circumstances, sometimes both. Fortunately, there is a book about America's political dynasties that helps explains what went wrong. If the Bushes reach three, they will be America's greatest political dynasty.

NINETEEN

The
Clinton
Dynasty

"[Bill Clinton] was a natural and he made it look too easy, and oh, how I hated him for that!"
—George H. W. Bush[1]

"I wonder how history is going to note our marriage."
—Hillary Rodham Clinton, to friend, mid-1980s[2]

C HARLOTTE CLINTON MEZVINSKY IS now too young to register to vote, but if she gets elected to the U.S. House of Representatives on November 6, 2040, the first day on which she will be constitutionally eligible to run, the new congresswoman-elect may wish to note that both her maternal and paternal grandparents once held high office in Washington.[3] Thus would Clinton-Mezvinsky join forty-eight families in American history that we designate "mix and match" political dynasties: three or more members joined through marriage, such as the Rockefellers with the Aldriches.

If Chelsea Clinton, Charlotte's mother, runs for office, as she suggests she might, and wins, she will be part of a dictionary-correct dynasty ("a succession of rulers of the same line of descent"), joining seventy-five other American families in which three members of the same name have held national office over more than one generation.

Bill Clinton and Hillary Rodham Clinton, Chelsea's parents and Charlotte's grandparents, being two people of the same generation, without their families having had elected officials in previous generations, are not a dynasty.

While Bill and Hillary await actions by their heirs to claim this distinction, journalists rush to mislabel them a dynasty. The media's temptation may be too great, especially when there is another great political family in need of a counterweight. Conflict between candidates is standard stuff; competing families multiply the opportunities for conflict, and when the conflicts have been ongoing for a quarter century of elections and have already involved three presidents, it's a great story line. Perhaps it's not surprising that the Clintons and the Bushes do not think highly of the press. During a White House transfer of power in 1992, Hillary and Barbara strolled the South Lawn toward a gaggle of reporters. "Avoid this crowd like the plague," Barbara advised. "That's right. I know that feeling already," Hillary agreed.[4]

THE DEMOCRATIC NATIONAL CONVENTION delegates who came to Madison Square Garden in New York City in 1992 were enthralled watching a grainy film of a teenager shaking hands with John F. Kennedy. Kennedy was the last president they loved; the young man, Bill Clinton, they had just nominated for president. It was as if the picture had been taken for this moment—which, in a sense, it had been. This was not a photo of a White House receiving line with each guest lined up to shake hands and keep moving. This was a Rose Garden event—July, 1963—in which 100 teenage boys were to gather in a semicircle below the speaker's podium. Sixteen-year-old Bill was fast off the bus. He surged forward with long strides—he was six foot three and weighed 200 pounds—and placed himself in the front row, fifteen feet from the president, the first to shake his hand. As it happened, when the president was murdered in November, Bill was positioned to recall that handshake at civics club luncheons in Hot Springs, Arkansas.[5]

Young Bill aimed for Washington: Georgetown University was the only school he applied to as a high school senior. Once in college he also studied firsthand the politics of Capitol Hill through a part-time clerk's job with one of his state's senators, J. William Fulbright. The senator, who had been a Rhodes Scholar at Oxford, encouraged him to seek that honor.

THE CLINTON DYNASTY—*A Selective Genealogy*

The Clinton background was rural lower middle class: a traveling sales-man father killed in a car accident before Bill was born, a mother the daugh-ter of the iceman in a small town named Hope, a stepfather who was an abusive alcoholic. What Bill had been born with, besides a modest rank-ing in the social order, was the oversized affability that often characterizes successful politicians and salesmen. What he acquired on his own was a first-class education at elite institutions and the connections this brings. At Georgetown and Oxford he made friends for life, some of whom would play prominent roles on his way to the presidency, some of whom he would ap-point to key positions once he got there. At Yale Law School he met Hillary Rodham.

There was always the thrust of a driving ambition. During the summer of 1972, while in law school, Bill worked for the McGovern presidential campaign in Texas. David Maraniss's wonderful biography tells of a lunch in a Mexican restaurant in Houston with a political organizer named Billy Carr. "'I'm gonna tell you something and you're gonna laugh,' Clinton said as he devoured a plate of enchiladas. 'As soon as I get out of school, I'm movin' back to Arkansas. I love Arkansas. I'm goin' back there to live. I'm gonna run for office there. And someday I'm gonna be governor. And then one day I'll be callin' ya, Billie, and tellin' ya I'm runnin' for president and I need your help.'"[6]

If the Clintons were ever to be a dynasty, Bill Clinton would be his own founding father. There was no Joseph Kennedy Sr. to direct and finance his path; no Bush brothers, sisters, and cousins to rally to his banner; no famous generals or Supreme Court justices to add weight to his résumé. If presidency backgrounds come in categories of Washington or Lincoln, there is no doubt which one Bill would fit in.

Perhaps young Hillary Rodham also wanted someday to run for president. She was raised in a middle-class suburb of Chicago where the neighbors dreamed of becoming richer than their present status, not of wielding political power. Yet as a teenager she became active in politics—and at a much younger age than Bill Clinton (or of any Bush when not campaigning for father). She read Barry Goldwater's *Conscience of a Conservative* approvingly, which pleased her father, who ran a small business making drapes for hotels, and adhered strongly to conservative positions on unions, government spending, and taxes. In the 1964 Goldwater presidential campaign, seventeen-year-old Hillary went door-to-door in tough Chicago neighborhoods, digging for information about Democratic voters that might help the campaign get them disqualified. "I liked Senator Goldwater because he was a rugged individualist who swam against the political tide," Hillary recalled, describing herself as "a Goldwater girl, right down to my cowgirl outfit and straw cowboy hat emblazoned with the slogan 'AuH2O.'"[7] At the same time, she carefully noted, "My active involvement in the First United Methodist Church of Park Ridge opened my eyes and heart to the needs of others and helped instill a sense of social responsibility rooted in my faith."[8]

By the time Hillary and Bill met in the Yale law library in 1971, she had gone through a gradual transformation from Goldwater Republican to Rockefeller Republican to "a mind conservative and a heart liberal," while Bill at Oxford had struggled with how to avoid being drafted into a war he opposed. Their different journeys had led them to a remarkably similar outlook. Bill's work on a failed senatorial campaign in Connecticut had left him frustrated with pure idealism; Hillary's defection to the Democrats was driven by her sense of social justice, but she had not left behind the pragmatism of her early conservative years. As Bill remembered, his first impressions were that "she was both idealistic and practical. . . . She was as tired as I was of our side getting beat and treating defeat as evidence of moral virtue and superiority."[9] Hillary was impressed with Clinton's abiding concern for his home state and its seemingly intractable economic and social problems. "He was rooted, and most of us were disconnected."[10]

THEY HAD BEEN DATING only a few weeks before their relationship became serious enough to begin guiding their lives. Hillary had lined up a summer internship at a law firm of leftist persuasion in Oakland, California. Bill had been offered a job as George McGovern's campaign coordinator for southern states. Suddenly fearful of losing Hillary, Bill gave up on "the political experience of a lifetime" and announced to Hillary that he wanted to follow her to the West Coast, if she would let him.[11] Hillary was deeply moved, after she got over her disbelief. She understood what Bill was giving up, even if it was just for a summer. Bill's decision established how serious their relationship had become in a short time and convinced Hillary that committing to this man didn't necessarily mean she had to give up any part of who she was, and a relationship could be a partnership.

This notion of partnership was a defining concept for the Clintons. Women had always been part of the shaping and motive force in politically active families, but essentially as wives and mothers. Nannie Lodge, wife of Henry Cabot Lodge Sr., was essential to keeping a Senate grandee grounded in a democracy. She called him "Pinky." Louisa Catherine Johnson, wife of John Quincy Adams, thought she was inadequate (her husband did not), and titled her attempt at an autobiography *The Adventures of a Nobody*. Some had added influence as skilled campaigners, such as Martha Bowers, Robert Taft's wife. Some had influence outside their roles as political wives—Eleanor Roosevelt, of course. A great many made tremendous personal sacrifices to support their husbands: Barbara Bush relocated countless times to support George H. W. Bush's career, and, she admitted, it took an emotional toll. Yet the role of women had to be constitutionally secondary until 1920, when the Nineteenth Amendment was ratified, and even after the right to vote was in the law, attitudes had to catch up. During the drafting of the Constitution, Abigail Adams instructed John that unless women's rights were also included, American women were "determined to foment a rebellion." She must have said this on a day he had other things on his mind.

It was Hillary's close friend Diane Blair, a professor at the University of Arkansas, who wrote the classic article "Over His Dead Body," explaining "that statistically at least, for women aspiring to serve in Congress, the best husband has been a dead husband, most preferably one serving in Congress at the time of his demise."[12] The "widow's succession" was intended to be a noncontroversial placeholder technique to avoid awkward intraparty fights. Huey Long's widow Rose served unobtrusively for nearly a year in the Senate before quietly retiring.

There weren't many models to guide Hillary's ambition. One of her heroes had been Margaret Chase Smith, a Republican from Maine who was the first woman to serve in both the House and the Senate. Her thirty-two-year career in Congress began with her taking over her husband's seat. Smith had been a successful business executive and leader of women's organizations in Maine, leaving her career behind to follow her congressional husband to Washington as his secretary. After his death, she was unopposed to replace him in a special election and then kept winning, generally by very large margins. This did not carry over in her bid for the Republican presidential nomination against Goldwater, in which she lost every primary she entered.

HILLARY AND BILL WERE married in the summer of 1975. He had lost a race for Congress the year before. According to the AP bureau chief in the state capital, however, "It became a foregone conclusion that he would hold state office soon."[13] And a year after their wedding, Bill was elected Arkansas attorney general. Hillary had previously lived in Washington, working for John Doar, chief counsel to the impeachment investigation of President Nixon, and in Cambridge, working for the Children's Defense Fund. She advised on legislation before Congress that concerned children and was building a substantial expertise in family law and children's rights. How comfortably would her past fit into her Arkansas present? What could be transplanted to Little Rock, and what must be filed for future reference? There was no roadmap for the kind of political and marital partnership that Bill and Hillary wanted to have. Many of their actions were halting and improvised.

She knew that she was not going to be the kind of politician's wife defined by socializing, networking, doing charitable work, and taking care of the kids. Of more immediate concern was the matter of Bill's meager salary as attorney general, $26,500 a year. His failed bid for Congress left him $40,000 in debt, and there were debts from law school as well. Hillary had not become a lawyer to make money, which she avoided during her years working for the Children's Defense Fund and as a legal aid lawyer. Reversing course, she now went to work at the Rose Law Firm, an institution to which reporters always seemed to attach the word "venerable," and one that had never before hired a woman as an associate. By 1979 she was a partner, making a lot more than Bill. Then too, there was how she chose to identify herself. When Bill was elected governor in 1978, cards and invitations from the governor's mansion came from Hillary Rodham. People were talking. One of Bill's closest advisers, Vernon Jordan, convinced her to adopt her husband's name: Hillary Rodham Clinton. "The only person who didn't ask me or even talk to me about my name was my husband. He said my name was my business."[14] But this was no small matter in a small southern state in the early 1980s.

By the time Bill ran for president, Hillary was a seasoned campaigner. Even before Arkansas, she had gone door-to-door for Goldwater, 1964; campaigned for McGovern in Texas when in law school, 1972; and been field coordinator for Jimmy Carter in Indiana, 1976. Still, her involvement in Bill's presidential campaign was controversial. She hired and ran her own campaign staff, rather than take orders from headquarters. This is not what candidates' wives were supposed to do. Charting new territory can be painful, in politics as in other businesses.

How does one audition for the role of a president's First Lady? Are there exceptions for First Ladies with a graduate degree? It was "an odd experience" to be "solely 'the wife of,'" she later remarked.[15] The role seemed to chafe at times, and the public got glimpses of her discomfort. She wasn't like Tammy Wynette ("Stand by your Man"); she wasn't going to stay home baking cookies and pouring tea. These statements were not intended to be taken out of context, but that context happened within a larger context of Hillary trying to adjust to being a "wife of" while the rest of the country had to adjust their expectations of what a First Lady should be.

When Bill gave a speech praising Hillary's work on family and children's law, and joked that a vote for him was tantamount to "buy one, get one free," he sent chills up the spines of those who feared a copresidency or, worse, an unelected Svengali. The Clintons had done well in finding useful ways to bring Hillary's policy interests into the governor's administration. But Washington was not Little Rock writ large, although some from Little Rock thought so, and the Clintons' partnership would be sorely tested.

AS THE PRESIDENT-ELECT BEGAN to structure his administration, Hillary proposed a symbolic way to define her role by locating her office in the

West Wing, the "business" side of the White House, rather than the East Wing, the "social" side, where previous First Ladies had maintained their staff. But when she intimated that she wanted the space typically given to the vice president, all the fears about a copresidency found new credibility, both inside and outside the White House. Although not intended for public consumption, this was a misstep, part of the chaos that characterized Clinton's transition to office. Yet Bill was utterly open about Hillary's role in the transition. Announcing his first cabinet appointments, he said, "She advised me on these decisions as she has on every other decision I've made in the last 20 years."[16]

What job was fitting for a restyled First Lady? The attorney general, for instance, was unavailable because of a law passed under Nixon to prevent a repeat of JFK's appointment of his brother. So instead, she and Bill agreed she would manage health care reform, the most sweeping and fraught item on the domestic agenda.

Friends had often characterized Bill as the dreamer, Hillary as the pragmatist; Bill as the sail, Hillary as the anchor. The two had embraced the model themselves, to some extent, and it had seemed to work. It got them to the White House, despite all the barbs of the campaign trail. When it came to health care reform, however, the balance they had achieved fell apart. Both were swept up in the grandness of the idea of universal coverage. Going before Congress, Bill displayed the pen he would use to veto any legislation that did not fully cover the 37 million Americans who lacked health care insurance. Bill and Hillary backed themselves into a corner and proclaimed they'd rather take their lumps than negotiate on this one point. Their proposal was too complex, presented too big a target for Republicans, and was too evocative of big government. The Clintons ended up never sending the health care bill to Congress, and Hillary's name was attached to Bill's biggest domestic defeat.

IF A "VAST RIGHT-WING conspiracy," as Hillary called it, had made it all up—an affair between Bill and an intern, taking place in the West Wing—the plot would have been brilliant. Hillary was such a source of strength, and her past defense of her husband had been so effective, that it was abundantly clear that taking down Bill *had* to involve also taking down Hillary—humiliating her to the point where this faith and loyalty to her husband turned into foolishness at best or a ruse to aid her ascent to power at worst. Of course, the vast right-wing conspiracy, if there ever was one, didn't have to fabricate the made-to-order Monica Lewinsky sex scandal that would diminish not only the president, but everyone around him. They didn't have to because they had Bill.

Instead of being driven from public life, however, Hillary chose to extend her public life. Instead of abandoning the partnership she had formed with Bill, she found ways to transform it to her advantage. This was made possible by the way she and Bill operated on several levels simultaneously. If one aspect of their relationship was damaged beyond repair, she had others available: "As his wife, I wanted to wring Bill's neck. But he was not only my husband, he was also my President, and I thought that, in spite of everything, Bill led America and the world in a way that I continued to support."[17] In August 1998, with Bill's confession of a host of lies and a shameful infidelity out in the open, Hillary wrote, "I hadn't decided whether to fight for my husband and my marriage, but I was resolved to fight for my President."[18]

Read a certain way, this sounds like lawyer-speak. Hillary had once been paid to research how to impeach President Nixon: "Everything I had learned from the Watergate investigation convinced me that there were no grounds to impeach Bill."[19] This tone turned out to be exactly where the public would end up, and Hillary unintentionally struck exactly the right posture during this unimaginably painful time.

There were as many eyes on her, watching carefully her reactions and parsing her words, as there were on Bill. If she had decided to leave him, or simply fall silent, it is unlikely President Clinton would have enjoyed some of the highest approval ratings of his presidency in the run-up to impeachment. On the other hand, if she had defended him as a person rather than defending merely his presidency, she would have convinced no one and would likely have helped feed the charge that she only put up with this philanderer because of the power the marriage imparted. At the same time, while being careful to separate the president from the man, her own emotional tone had to hit just the right note. Sydney Blumenthal, their journalist defender, observed that "Hillary had to walk a fine line" somewhere between appearing to be either "a warrior or a wounded bird,"[20] while fully aware that her humiliation was the topic of millions of conversations, slanders, and off-color jokes.

The public's preference for Hillary's stance became even more evident in the public's indignant reaction to Kenneth Starr's soft-core report. The inclusion of minute detail—involving cigars, thongs, and bodily fluids—quickly came to be seen in the terms that Hillary had set out. It was an attack on the man, not the president. After watching Hillary (not previously known for exhibiting grace under pressure) react with dignity and renewed focus on the bigger picture rather than her own pain, it was easy to believe that Starr's constant harping on sexual deviance was a petty attack on the president's character.

If Starr's intention all along, as some of his staff would later admit, had been to destroy Bill Clinton and his activist First Lady, the greatest irony of the sordid tale was that he helped ensure the Clintons would not leave the national stage at the end of Bill's second term. Hillary's skyrocketing popularity brought pressure from fellow Democrats to enter the New York Senate race. Her preference had once been to find a job that involved policy but not politics. An academic setting like a think tank would do nicely. Now, a move to private life seemed tantamount to surrender. As the Senate voted on articles of impeachment, a vote Hillary was certain would come up short, she was, at that moment, pouring over a map of New York State with a trusted adviser, laying the groundwork for what someday might be a Clinton dynasty.

RUNNING FOR THE U.S. Senate from New York was a Kennedy gift to Hillary. What Bobby had proved was that electoral magnetism trumps being native-born and -bred in a state this large and diverse. It was not like Arkansas where everyone worth trusting comes from Arkansas (unless you're a Rockefeller). And the size of her Empire State victory—55 percent to the Republican's 43 percent—was impressive enough to give her additional elbow room on Capitol Hill. But what she did with this opportunity surprised those used to thinking of her as a partisan combatant. In the highly polarized environment of George W. Bush's presidency, this highly polarizing and outspoken figure opted to work quietly and seek bipartisan opportunities, even with those who had once been sworn enemies. House Majority Leader Tom DeLay, Republican from Texas, had walked out on President Clinton during a State of the Union address and later had helped lead the drive for impeachment. Now Senator Clinton and Representative DeLay worked together on issues related to foster care. On the Republican side, criticism of Hillary was largely limited to her positions on the issues at hand; hardly a whisper was heard about Whitewater, Rose Law Firm associations, Monica Lewinsky, or health care reform. Hillary, meanwhile, felt free to coyly reference her polarizing qualities, as when she praised De-

Caption TK
CREDIT TK

Lay's work while appearing on stage with him, and hastened to add that she wasn't sure her praise was helping the congressman with folks back home.[21]

She also avoided rekindling the old rivalry between the Bushes and the Clintons at a time when Bill and George 41were building a cordial friendship in the ex-presidents club. She may, however, have found George 43's appeal to presidential prerogative too appealing when she voted to authorize the use of force in Iraq, a vote that may well have cost her the presidential nomination in 2008.

Iraq, the most prominent and memorable aspect of the Bush legacy, bled over into the Clinton legacy with that vote. Hillary was uncharacteristically awkward in her attempts to explain her support for the resolution in 2008, claiming that the vote was for diplomacy, that it was intended to give the president a free hand, and that the intelligence was convincing. She resisted calling her vote a grave mistake until 2015, when preparing for a second run at the Democratic presidential nomination. "Over the years that followed, many Senators came to wish they had voted against the resolution. I was one of them. As the war dragged on, with every letter I sent to a family in New York who had lost a son or daughter, a father or mother, my mistake became more painful."[22]

THE YEAR 2008 SHOULD have been a great year for Hillary Rodham Clinton, Democrat. The game of presidential succession determined that this was destined to be her party's year in that the Republicans had been in office for eight years. Since the Constitution established a two-term limit in 1951, no party has won three straight elections, with only one exception: Republicans Ronald Reagan (1980, 1984) and George H.W. Bush (1988). The informal rule is that the candidate of the "out" party wins after the "in" party has been elected and reelected, thus chalking up two wins. It's not just that the Constitution limits how long a president can serve, it's that the voters don't seem to want a president's party to stay longer either. So in 2008, two-term president George W. Bush, Republican, was retiring and Hillary Clinton, Democrat, wasthe front-runner to succeed him. In 1992, President George H. W. Bush had been "in" and Bill Clinton was the "out" running against him. Bush 41 should have won reelection under this formula, but didn't; Democrat Clinton then served eight years and was succeeded in 2000 by Bush 43, Republican. The Clintons and the Bushes and their tag-team expectations were excellent fodder for talk radio and cable networks. But this political parlor game of in and out is only about which party is most likely to win a presidential election and isn't meant to help predict which candidate within each party is advantaged, as Hillary Clinton, Barack Obama, John Edwards, Joe Biden, and others would find out.

Early polls, as expected, showed Hillary well in the lead. She announced her candidacy in a videotaped message, sitting on a couch, telling her supporters, "I'm in. And I'm in to win," which to some smacked of entitlement. Moreover, her major opponent, Barack Obama, barely had a toehold in national politics, having been elected to the Senate in 2004. If voters needed added reason to want Hillary, wasn't it about time for a woman chief executive? The world was full of remarkable examples: India's Indira Gandhi, Israel's Golda Meir, Margaret Thatcher of the United Kingdom, Germany's Angela Merkel. It was embarrassing that the United States still had not had a woman president. "I am not running as a woman. I am running because I believe I am the best qualified and experienced person," Hillary told audiences in her standard campaign speech.

While she was not a natural campaigner like Bill, the happy warrior, she had proved herself by winning two Senate races. Yet when Obama in debate said she was "likable enough," it wasn't difficult for voters to understand this faint praise. What was difficult was why she ran such a bad campaign. Bill's 1996 presidential campaign had been flawless. Subsequent analyses found that her staff seemed to spend more energy feuding than assisting.[23] So much money was squandered that she ultimately had to lend $5 million to her own cause. Also Bill could be a problem. He responded badly when his wife came under attack, particularly when he tried to marginalize Obama's key win in the South Carolina primary by comparing it to victories by Jesse Jackson.

The voter turnout for both Hillary and Obama was record-breaking in the primary states, but it was the rookie Obama campaign that figured out how to win where delegates were selected in caucuses. Hillary's finest speech came in June, after she had essentially lost the nomination, when she gathered her disheartened workers in Washington. "Although we weren't able to shatter that highest, hardest glass ceiling this time, thanks to you, it's got about 18 million cracks in it," she said to roaring applause. "And the light is shining through like never before, filling us all with the hope and the sure knowledge that the path will be a little easier next time."

So Barack Obama, candidate of the "out" party, became president of the United States and chose his rival for the nomination to be his secretary of state. Of all the ways in which Hillary Clinton could have served his administration, foreign policy seemed at first blush to be the least likely. She had wanted to be Bill's primary domestic policy adviser, and often was just that, even if informally. Yet aside from actions in the Balkans, the Clinton administration could point to few major foreign policy successes. Hillary herself could not have been more surprised by Obama's offer, especially since one of the major points of contention between them had been over a foreign policy vote she made in the Senate. On the other hand, she was one of the most recognizable figures in the world, had proved both her loyalty and independence, and, as president-elect Obama remarked, was "a sign to friend and foe of the seriousness of my commitment to renew American diplomacy."[24] Hillary would serve in the cabinet only for Obama's first term. Her relations with the president were generally reported in the press as good, but not close. Her relations with the secretary of defense, often an area of discord in other administrations, also received high marks. Mostly the media followed her vast travels. She visited 112 countries as secretary of state, which may have been a record.

When she first joined the Obama government, inside Washington predictions were that Bill Clinton, in wide-ranging retirement, would be a "distraction" to the president and his secretary of state. This did not come to pass. The former president was eager to support his wife by keeping a lower profile in matters that concerned her. The press then largely drew comparisons that worked in Hillary's favor, such as "Hillary . . . is not to be confused with Bill. She is a workhorse, not a show pony."[25]

BILL CLINTON STARTED HIS ex-presidency by doing the two things that are required of all presidents when leaving the White House: he wrote an account of his achievements in office and built a presidential library. He did these in Clintonesque fashion. His memoir, *My Life*, was 955 pages long (plus another 42 pages of acknowledgments and index). His library building was a dramatic span across the Arkansas River, the largest presidential library in terms of physical space, with the largest archives and full-scale replicas of the Oval Office and Cabinet Room. It was also the most expensive, costing $165 million in private funding.

At first, writing a book and building a library kept him busy. But by ex-president standards he was young, in his mid-fifties, with the hope of being an ex-president for many years. The people he cared most about were presently engaged: Hillary was busy being a senator; Chelsea was busy at school, first at Stanford, then at Oxford. He spent a lot of time giving speeches, and since his celebrity initially was in direct proportion to his distance from the United States, it was in faraway places that he made the largest sums of money. Ultimately, his presidency would gain weight with time and comparison, and he began making more speeches at home.

Yet his friends and staff could see that something grander had to be found to fill the space in his life. This was to be the Clinton Foundation, originally put in place to raise funds for the presidential library but soon expanding to focus on improving crop yields in Africa, providing earthquake relief in Haiti, reducing the cost of AIDS drugs, helping small businesses in Harlem, preserving forests in Tierra del Fuego, and whatever else seemed worthwhile to the restless former president. A Bill Gates can do such wonderful things with his own money. Bill Clinton, of the partnership that

Hillary had once called "dead broke," had to figure out how to leverage his remarkable glitter to lure money for his agenda of wonderful things.

His solution was an annual conference, called the Clinton Global Initiative, which rivaled the famous Davos gatherings as the place to tell the wealthy and powerful how they should spend their philanthropic money. There was no master plan. As was Bill Clinton's nature, the agenda was created piece by piece from his wanderings and conversations. What fun, Clinton-style, to bring together Bono, Mick Jagger, and Angelina Jolie with Carlos Slim, a Mexican billionaire, or Frank Giustra, a Canadian billionaire, as well as the people who give out the money at Goldman Sachs and Starbucks!

Three *Washington Post* reporters—David A. Fahrenthold, Tom Hamburger, and Rosalind S. Helderman—published a stunning article in June, 2015, that captured the massive structure of the ex-president's invention. "Today, the Clinton Foundation is unlike anything else in the history of the nation and, perhaps, the world. It is a global philanthropic empire run by a former U.S. president and closely affiliated with a potential future president, with the audacious goal of solving some of the world's most vexing problems by bringing together the wealthiest, glitziest and most powerful people from every part of the planet." The reporters called Bill Clinton "a convener who wrangles rich people's money for poor people's problems." "The foundation now includes 11 major initiatives, . . . has raised $2 billion, employs more than 2,000 people and has a combined annual budget of more than $223 million."[26] By the Clinton Foundation's accounting, it has benefited at least 430 million people in more than 180 countries. There are critics. Some are concerned about contributions from foreign governments, such as Saudi Arabia and Qatar, and corporations. Is getting them to "do good" sufficient reward, or are there implicit strings attached? Others raise questions relating to Bill's speaking fees and about the Clintons' entourage, such as media reports that Sidney Blumenthal was being paid $10,000 a month starting in 2009 to advise the foundation on a project to promote Clinton's presidential legacy. The Clintons have heard it all before. As a *Washington Post* editorial notes, "The Clintons have long been haunted by criticism of their ethical behavior."[27]

In mid-2015 the future of the foundation became the immediate problem of a new CEO, Donna Shalala, the retiring University of Miami president, who had served as secretary of Health and Human Services through the eight years of the Clinton presidency. The foundation, Shalala noted, is smaller than other institutions she has run. She told *The Chronicle of Philan-*

thropy, "I love messy institutions." By "messy," she said she meant institutions that are "complex and multidimensional."[28] Shalala raised $3 billion for the University of Miami. Besides the standard problems that always follow in the wake of the Clintons, Shalala must now figure out how the foundation can survive and prosper beyond Bill Clinton's lifetime.

A Fable for Our Times

If Bill Clinton in his youth had rescued a genie from a bottle, and the genie had then granted him three wishes, his first wish would be to become president of the United States. The wish would be granted unless he was greedy and asked to be a great president since it was beyond the genie's power to place Bill in crisis times, like Washington's, Lincoln's, or FDR's. His second wish might be something spicy. For young Bill had a massive appetite, as had his hero, Jack Kennedy, who was fortunate to live in less transparent times. What might be the last wish? If Bill had rescued the genie at an older age, say, in his early sixties, would he not wish to be surrounded by worshipful billionaires, world leaders, and movie stars, all eager to seek his advice? The genie would then give him the Clinton Foundation.

ANY ACCOUNT OF BILL and Hillary Clinton—even an account of them as politicians—needs the importance of their daughter in their lives. In no presidential memoir is a child as constant a reference as Chelsea is in Bill Clinton's *My Life*. Harry Truman also had an only child, a daughter, and his love for Margaret was deeply felt. President Truman wrote as many words about his presidency as President Clinton did about his. But Truman's two volumes mention Margaret only eighteen times, and nothing more personal than one letter Harry wrote to his mother shortly after he became president: "A guard has to go with Bess and Margaret everywhere they go—and they don't like it. They both spend a lot of time figuring how to beat the game, but it just can't be done."[29] Chelsea appears eighty-one times in her father's book, starting with her birth. Indeed, Hillary's *Living History* also writes of their daughter's birth—the same event—but from a different perspective.

Bill's Account of Chelsea's Birth

Hillary was pregnant—very pregnant. We badly wanted to have a child and had been trying for some time without success. In the summer of 1979, we decided to make an appointment with a fertility expert in San Francisco as soon as we got back from a short vacation in Bermuda, but we had a wonderful time, so wonderful we never made it to San Francisco. Soon after we got home, Hillary found out she was pregnant. . . . A few weeks before her delivery date, Hillary was having a few problems. Her doctor told her she absolutely couldn't travel. . . . Unfortunately, that meant she couldn't go with me to the annual Washington meeting of the National Governors Association, including dinner at the White House with President and Mrs. Carter. I went to the conference . . . and returned as soon as I could on the night of February 27.

Fifteen minutes after I walked into the Governor's Mansion, Hillary's water broke, three weeks early. I was nervous as a cat. . . . The state troopers who worked at the mansion . . . got us to the hospital in no time. Soon after we arrived, we learned Hillary would have to give birth by cesarean section because the baby was "in breech," upside down in the womb. I was told that hospital policy did not permit fathers in the delivery room. . . . I pleaded with the hospital administrator to let me go in. . . . [Hillary] needed me there. They relented. At 11:24 p.m., I held Hillary's hand and looked over the screen blocking her view of the cutting and bleeding to see the doctor lift our baby out of her body. It was the happiest moment of my life.[30]

Hillary's Account of Chelsea's Birth

As my March due date drew near, my doctor said I couldn't travel, which meant that I missed the annual White House dinner for the Governors. Bill got back to Little Rock on Wednesday, February 27, in time for my water to break. That threw him and the state troopers into a panic. Bill ran around with the Lamaze list of what to take to the hospital. It recommended bringing a small plastic bag filled with ice, to suck on during labor. As I hobbled to the car, I saw a state trooper loading a thirty-nine-gallon black garbage bag filled with ice into the trunk.

After we arrived at the hospital, it became clear that I would have to have a cesarean, not something we had anticipated. Bill requested that the hospital permit him to accompany me into the operating room, which was unprecedented. He told the administrators that he had gone with his mother to see operations and knew he'd be fine. That he was the Governor certainly helped convince Baptist Hospital to let him in. . . .

Our daughter's birth was the most miraculous and awe-inspiring event in my life. Chelsea Victoria Clinton arrived three weeks early on February 27, 1980, at 11:24 P.M., to the great joy of Bill and our families. While I was recovering, Bill took Chelsea in his arms for father-daughter "bonding" laps around the hospital. He would sing to her, rock her, show her off and generally suggest that he had invented fatherhood.[31]

IN 1981 AND 1982, when Chelsea Clinton was two and three years old, her father was between elections as governor. Otherwise, from her birth until well into college, she lived in public housing. It is different, and at times difficult, to be the governor's child; certainly even more so if your father is president. Perhaps still more if you are an only child. Teddy Roosevelt's clan had a wonderful time with each other in the White House. The Kennedy children had lots of cousins. But the history of many dynastic children, as we have seen, has often been sad, even tragic. Teenage years can be tough, but this does not seem to have been the case for Chelsea. There are lots of reasons why, of course: her own strength, personality, and talent; key decisions of her parents, such as sending her to a private school in Washington—criticized by many Americans—but which allowed Chelsea to avoid the TV cameras and reporters that were a part of Amy Carter's life at a public school; grandparents and close family friends who sometimes were there when Bill and Hillary were not. Even, in fact, understanding reporters in the White House press corps.

But another reason may be public housing: metaphorically, being politically special, virtually from birth, creates a range of experiences that can turn the exceptional into the ordinary. When do you know which of your classmates are true friends and which are the ones who just want to hang out at the governor's mansion? What gifts are appropriate, and which are over the top? Is there public behavior that children without famous parents do not have to learn but for those like Chelsea is best learned young? These are lessons FDR's children never learned. During the 1986 governor's campaign, according to Hillary, "Bill and I tried to prepare Chelsea for what she might hear about her father or, for that matter, about her mother. We sat around our dinner table in the Governor's Mansion role-playing with her, pretending we were in debates where one of us acted like a political opponent who criticized Bill for not being a good Governor."[32] This was role-playing for a six-year-old, a lesson plan not otherwise available in first grade. Chelsea was about to turn thirteen when the family moved to the White House.

There is in Bill's memoir a palpable sense of pride in his daughter. "Garcia Marquez lavished most of his attention on Chelsea, who said she had read two of his books. He later told me that he didn't believe a fourteen-year-old could understand his work, so he launched into an extended discussion with her about *One Hundred Years of Solitude*. He was so impressed that he later sent her an entire set of his novels. . . . I was struck by the attention [Nelson Mandela] paid to Chelsea. In the eight years I was in the White House, he never talked to me without asking about her." Bill even cites his daughter's Stanford senior thesis on the Irish peace process.[33] There is the repeated sense of Chelsea's presence, even when it raises questions or is unprecedented. The First Lady is expected to travel abroad representing the United States. But is the First [Teenage] Daughter? "On March 25, Hillary began her first extended overseas trip without me, a twelve-day visit to Pakistan, India, Nepal, Bangladesh, and Sri Lanka. She took Chelsea along on what would be an important effort for the United States and a grand personal odyssey for them both. . . . Hillary met me in Moscow. She brought Chelsea, too, because we didn't want her to be alone right after Mother's death. Staying together in the guest quarters of the Kremlin and seeing Moscow in the dead of winter would be a good distraction for all of us. . . . In the middle of the month, Hillary and Chelsea left for Lillehammer, Norway, to represent America at the Winter Olympics. . . . On the twenty-second, Chelsea and I flew to Bulgaria, which I was the first American President to visit. . . . Chelsea traveled to Okinawa with me [for the G-8 meeting]. . . . In the streets of Cartagena [Colombia], Chelsea and I danced [with a group of young musicians]. . . . A few days later, Chelsea and I went to Brunei for the annual APEC summit. . . . On July 11, I opened a summit with Ehud Barak and Yasser Arafat at Camp David in an attempt to resolve the remaining obstacles to peace. . . . And Chelsea stayed with me the whole time, entertaining our guests and helping me deal with the endless hours of tension."[34] This is a sampling of Chelsea sightings and activities and doesn't include visits to Buckingham Palace, the terra cotta warriors at Xi'n, the Great Wall, the Forbidden City, Shanghai, the Taj Mahal, Morocco, Ephesus, the Acropolis, Istanbul, Vietnam, and Africa.

DURING THE LONG, AGONIZING run-up to Bill Clinton's impeachment, while all eyes were on Hillary, Chelsea was the subject of much less scrutiny. Even Hillary, with all her simmering anger toward the press, felt it did the right thing by giving Chelsea a pass. One image, however, from this time is striking. It was just after the revelation that Bill had been lying, Chelsea was home from Stanford, and the family was on its way to Martha's Vineyard. Hillary had not yet fully decided she would stay with Bill, although she likely knew there wasn't another course. Hillary wore dark sunglasses as they walked across the lawn toward the waiting helicopter, and Chelsea stood between them, holding a hand of each parent, serving as both a buffer and a link.

CHELSEA GRADUATED FROM STANFORD in 2001 with highest honors in history. In 2003 she completed an M.Phil. in international relations at Oxford. In 2010 she completed a master's degree in public health at Columbia University. She was awarded a D.Phil. from Oxford in 2014, doing her doctoral work while living in New York. She has worked for the consulting firm McKinsey & Company and the hedge fund Avenue Capital Group. For nearly three years she was a special correspondent for NBC, reportedly with an annual salary of $600,000. As with the young Bushes at a comparable age, her name seemed to be useful on the job market. In 2010 she married Marc Mezvinsky, who had given her a tour of Stanford when she was choosing a college. He worked at Goldman Sachs for eight years before cofounding Eaglevale Partners, a macro fund that tries to make a profit from global and economic trends, such as the "sustainable recovery" of Greece. His roughly $400 million fund is considered modest by Wall Street standards. Like anyone connected to the Clintons (or the Bushes), his investors are of interest to the media.[35] The public is also kept informed of basic facts: Marc and Chelsea bought a Manhattan condominium in 2013 for $10.5 million, ensuring that Chelsea will never be accused of being a carpetbagger in New York; her daughter, Charlotte Clinton Mezvinsky was born on September 26, 2014; Chelsea signed a contract to write a book, aimed at readers ages ten to fourteen, to be titled, "It's Your World: Get Informed, Get Inspired & Get Going," to be published in 2015.

WILL CHELSEA FOLLOW IN the family business? Some can hardly wait. One *Politico* headline in 2015 read, "Excited for Jeb and Hillary? Just Wait for Chelsea vs. George P."

In 2013, Chelsea told CNN that she would consider running for public office, just "not now." To Jon Stewart, she limited her avoidance of politics to "this point in my life." Her father isn't being so taciturn. He sees the White House going naturally to Hillary, but "over the long run, Chelsea." Explaining why she should be president, he remarked, "She knows more than we do about everything."[36] She has already proved herself an energetic campaigner when speaking at a hundred colleges on behalf of her mother in 2008. Young audiences found her engaging, sometimes frank. Asked whether her mom would do better than her dad in office, she answered, "Yes, I do think she'll be a better president." When a student at a town hall-style meeting asked whether Hillary's standing had been diminished by her father's affair, she replied, "Wow. You're the first person actually that's ever asked me that question in the, I don't know, maybe 70 college campuses I've now been to." She then added, "And I do not think that it's any of your business."[37]

Running for office is a high-risk option. Do mothers start running for office on the same timeline as their husbands? When and under what circumstances do voters tire of a dynasty? How long a family can stay on top was a painful question for the Adamses. The Bushes kept losing elections and kept coming back. But it hurts. There is useful work that hurts less, such as a Kennedy becoming an ambassador or Eleanor Roosevelt at the United Nations. Some of the Tafts and Breckinridges moved on to superior achievement in education.

For Chelsea there is another option that must be tempting. The William J. Clinton Foundation changed its name in 2013. It is now the Bill, Hillary & Chelsea Clinton Foundation. Someday it can be hers to run, a challenge of great opportunity. Her parents have been a remarkable partnership for over forty years, and with continuing expectations. But sooner or later there will be a new sign on the storefront: "Clintons & Daughter."

EPILOGUE

ENDING IN MID-SENTENCE

THE WRITERS OF FICTION are blessed with the option of concluding "The End." The writers whose subjects keep moving do not have this luxury. *America's Political Dynasties: From Adams to Kennedy*, published in 1966, ended in mid-sentence. So that we all start at the same place, here is the book's last page, numbered for annotation.

In charting the future of the Kennedys, all who know them well agree that Teddy, despite Senate seniority, will defer to his older brother. The dynasty's hierarchy is rigid. But what will Bobby seek? After Jack won the presidential nomination he presented his campaign manager with a cigarette box. Inscribed across the lid:

ROBERT F. KENNEDY
When I'm Through, How About You?
Democratic National Convention
Los Angeles, 1960.[176]

A joke that made the rounds during the early days of the Kennedy Administration went: "We'll have Jack for eight years, Bobby for eight, and Teddy for eight. Then it'll be 1984." Such arithmetical tinkering was thrown out of balance by Jack Kennedy's death. Now there are many imponderables—Lyndon Johnson's health, his successes and failures as President, Hubert Humphrey's ambition, the mood of the country, war and peace, prosperity and recession, acts of God and man. But in any political timetable age weighs heavily in the Kennedys' favor. Most American presidents have been in their fifties. The precocious brothers Kennedy will be factors in politics for many years to come.

Presidential Election Years	Bob's Age	Ted's Age
1968	43	36
1972	47	40
1976	51	44
1980	55	48
1984	59	52
1988	63	56
1992	67	60

And in 1992 Joseph P. Kennedy III, Bobby's eldest son, will be forty, the age at which his uncle Jack started his drive for the presidency; John F. Kennedy, Jr., will be thirty, the same age as Uncle Teddy was when he entered the Senate.

Rose and Joe Kennedy have twenty-four grandchildren, thirteen named Kennedy. The youngsters are being raised in much the same manner as were their parents. Politics is bred into them. When Bobby's daughter Kathleen wanted to stop her younger brother from being naughty in a department store, she chose her words wisely. "Joe," she commanded, "do be quiet. You are losing votes acting like this!"[177]

Eunice Kennedy Shriver told a Chicago newspaperwoman in 1960, "All we talk about is winning." Then she picked up her infant son Timothy, held him aloft, and gently began his indoctrination: "Win, win, win."[178]

1. Robert Kennedy was killed while seeking the Democratic presidential nomination, June 6, 1968.

2. Ted Kennedy sought the Democratic presidential nomination in 1980, and his loss is generally attributed to the "Chappaquiddick incident," July 18, 1969; he died August 25, 2009.

3. Joseph P. Kennedy (b. 1952) was a member of the U.S. House of Representatives, 1987–99; he chose not to seek the Massachusetts governorship in 1998, after a messy divorce.

4. John F. Kennedy Jr., an inexperienced pilot, died July 16, 1999, when his plane crashed into the Atlantic near Martha's Vineyard, Massachusetts.

5. Kathleen Kennedy Townsend was lieutenant governor of Maryland, 1995–2003, and then defeated when she ran for governor in 2002.

6. Eunice Kennedy Shriver was the founder of the Special Olympics; she died August 11, 2009.

7. Timothy Shriver, chairman of the Special Olympics, has never sought public office. He has a PhD in education. He is the author of *Fully Alive: Discovering What Matters Most*, about his work with disabled athletes in which he devotes a chapter to his Aunt Rosemary, President Kennedy's sister, and how her father, Joseph Kennedy Sr., had her lobotomized.

In the presidential election of 2016, the American people elected